Discovering Oregon's
Wilderness
Areas

Donna Lynn Ikenberry

Discovering Oregon's

Wilderness Areas

Donna Lynn Ikenberry

Frank **A**mato

PORTLAND

DEDICATION

For My Brother And My Friend,
DON DEE IKENBERRY

ACKNOWLEDGMENTS

There are numerous highlights in seeing one's words in print; perhaps the most exciting for me is being able to dedicate the finished product to someone special. In this case, that someone special is my brother, Don Ikenberry.

Don is more than just a brother, he's a special friend too, one of the greatest guys on the planet, one who has often been the friend I needed most. He's also a staunch supporter; always there to encourage me, to praise my efforts, to remind me again and again that someday I'll be rewarded for all my efforts.

I must also give thanks to God. I'm grateful to Her (or Him) for the opportunity to witness everything from the penguins of Antarctica, to the beauty of Oregon's Wilderness Areas. In the wilderness, I've stood atop many a mountain peak, completely awed by the scenes around me. Camped in the forest, I've been lulled to sleep by raging rivers, trickling streams, and plummeting waterfalls. And I can't forget the times I've observed a rainbow of wildflowers sprinkled across an alpine slope, heard the forceful scream of a red-tailed hawk, or seen the saucer-like eyes of a newborn fawn.

The blessings continue as I express my gratitude to my family, whom I thank God for each day. I am truly enriched by them as their support has no end; their love is unconditional, it has no bounds, and their strength is unwavering. A special thank you goes to my mom, Beverly Bruer Ikenberry, my dad, Don Ikenberry, my brother and his wife, Don Ikenberry and Yolie Gutierrez, and my youngest brother David and his family, Laura, Andrew, and Sarah Ikenberry.

The newest member of my family is my best pal and life partner, Mike Vining. I am grateful for the day we met atop the highest peak in Texas, and continue to be amazed by his love, understanding, generosity, kindness, goodness, patience, dedication, and desire to be doing something in the great outdoors.

Friends are so very important to me and I am blessed with many extraordinary ones. Too many to mention, you know who you are, both my friends of many years and my new ones. I thank you for adding so much love and joy to my life.

In gathering trail information, there are a couple of government agencies—the U.S. Forest Service and the Bureau of Land Management—to acknowledge.

In addition, I must acknowledge several outdoor companies who provided necessities ranging from a pedometer, hiking boots, backpack, day pack, tent, and waterproof jackets and pants, to cold-weather mitts. Thank you Avocet, Columbia Sportswear, Danner, Hi-Tec, Jansport, Kelty, Nikwax, North Face, Outdoor Research, Pedco, Performance, and Solstice.

And last, but never least, a sincere blessing must go to Frank Amato and the other folks at Frank Amato Publications. Thanks again for a job well done.

WARNING

ALWAYS BE PREPARED WHEN HIKING FOR WEATHER
CHANGES AND TRAIL CHANGES. NATURE CONTINUALLY
PROVIDES VARIETY, CHALLENGE, AND DANGER.
BE PREPARED!

Published in 1998 by:
Frank Amato Publications, Inc.
PO Box 82112 • Portland, Oregon 97282 • (503) 653-8108

Softbound ISBN: 1-57188-132-8 Softbound UPC: 0-66066-00332-4

All Photographs taken by the author
Cover photo: Sky Lakes Wilderness.

Book Design: Tony Amato

Printed in Canada

1 3 5 7 9 10 8 6 4 2

TABLE OF CONTENTS

INTRODUCTION

OREGON IS A LAND OF DIVERSITY, A STATE BLESSED WITH ONE OF THE world's most beautiful coastlines, a potpourri of Pacific Ocean, rugged cliffs, lofty seastacks, and abundant wildlife. East of the Pacific lies the Coast Range, a lush mix of plants, old-growth forest, and endangered species. Still further are the green, fertile valleys where most of the population lives and where many of the crops are grown. Continue the trek east and there's the mighty Cascade Mountains, a robust range extending from northern California to southern Canada. Next, the Beaver State is a land of sagebrush and desert, with many distinctive mountain ranges bobbing upon the rich ranchland of the east.

There's no doubt that Oregon's landscape is stunning and diverse. Fortunately, it's wilderness areas are just as distinct. Here, more than 2,100,000 acres of designated wilderness are managed in 36 individual areas. (There's a 37th area, the nation's smallest and least accessible wilderness, that I didn't cover here. Oregon Islands bobs off the Oregon coast, comprised of 485 acres and 56 islands/groups.)

Wilderness areas range from the tall granite peaks, high mountain lakes, and rushing streams of the Eagle Cap Wilderness, located in the Wallowa Mountains, to the quiet, lush, 800-year-old western redcedars of the Waldo Lake Wilderness. It also offers everything from a trek into the depths of Hells Canyon, the deepest gorge in North America, to a rock climb up the 300-foot pinnacles of the Menagerie Wilderness, to the glaciers and 11,237-foot summit of Mt. Hood, Oregon's highest peak.

What is wilderness? You may wonder. To some folks the word "wilderness" means a trip to the city park, ice chests crammed full of goodies, baseball gloves and bats ready for action. To others, wilderness may signify a drive through Yellowstone National Park in bumper-to-bumper traffic.

To me, wilderness is a unique experience whereby one hikes through the woods or above timberline, enjoying the peace and solitude of an uncrowded land. Here, I may touch a delicate wildflower and watch for signs of birds, mammals, and other plant or animal species. Or, I may just sit and relax by a singing stream, watching the world go by.

Regardless of each individual interpretation of "wilderness," wilderness as defined in this book is subject to those areas designated by Congress as a result of the Wilderness Act of 1964. (Currently there are more than 104 million acres of wilderness, more than half of which exists in Alaska.)

In 1956 the first wilderness bill was introduced in Congress by Hubert Humphrey, then the Democratic senator for Minnesota. Also supporting Humphrey was John P. Saylor, a Republican House Member from Pennsylvania, and nine co-sponsors. In 1964, after nearly twenty hearings, the bill was finally passed. According to the law, wilderness "shall be administered for the use and enjoyment of the American people in such a manner as will leave them unimpaired for future use and enjoyment as wilderness, and so as to provide for the protection of these areas (and) the preservation of their wilderness character."

But "wilderness character" is becoming much more difficult to protect. Why? Because, we are loving the wilderness to death. Many areas suffer because of overcrowding. Unfortunately, people flock together instead of spreading out. And many times, we travel familiar trails instead of exploring someplace new.

Although solitude can be found in the majority of wilderness areas, some areas are attractive to too many people, with overcrowding a growing problem. And the problem is expected to increase in severity. In his book, *Battle For The Wilderness*, author Michael Frome states that as of 1974 the government was forecasting a wilderness use increase of 1,000 percent by the year 2000.

The need to preserve and protect areas such as these are far greater than one might imagine. In a world filled with black-topped roads, cemented cities, and crowds, it is comforting to know that small pockets of natural land have been set aside to enjoy. Can you really blame the folks who are anxious to escape from the city and visit a land of pristine beauty? Of course not! But something must be done to protect the human race from loving the land to death.

There are many do's and do not's in relation to managing a wilderness. Primitive methods of travel are allowed. You may backpack, day hike, ride a horse, or pack in with your favorite animal such as: a horse, mule, llama, or even a backpacking dog. But, motorcycles, mountain bikes, and other mechanical or motorized methods of travel are not allowed.

Some wilderness visitors do not agree with the policy, but mining and cattle grazing are allowed in some areas. As long as a mining claim is valid, mining is allowed, but with rules and regulations that must be adhered to. Also, cattle grazing is allowed if cattle were grazing on the land prior to the area becoming a designated wilderness. Again, certain rules apply.

But basically the wilderness is a place, "where man is a visitor who does not remain," and a place where visitors are asked to, "take only pictures; leave only footprints." To permit others the same wonderful experience that you might find in the wilderness please remember the following:

1. "Take only pictures, leave only footprints" are six words that everyone should remember. It is against the law to pick flowers or to remove Indian artifacts. If you want to remember a special moment, a precious flower, a monstrous mushroom, take photographs. And leave footprints only on the trails. Do not make trails wider by skirting around the drier edges of a muddy trail. Plow right through. Don't take short-cuts.
2. All backpackers should carry a portable camp stove. Everyone loves a nice warm campfire, but if wood is scarce please use a stove. If you do build a fire use existing fire rings and be sure your campfire is dead out.
3. If everyone would pack out what they pack in wouldn't the world be a lot cleaner place to live? Please pack out all of your garbage. Do not bury garbage as wild animals will dig it up. If you burn your garbage remember foil and cans don't burn. Carry them out.
4. Those packing into the wilderness will find a 10 or 12 person/animal group limit consisting of, for example, 6 people, 6 pack animals, or 8 people, 4 pack animals. Stock owners should note that feed should be carried into the wilderness. Also, animals should be picketed at least 200 feet from any water source. And hikers should remain on the down side of the trail when horseback riders or packers meet on the trail.
5. Fishing and hunting permits are required.

6. Although dogs are allowed in all of Oregon's wilderness areas many object to them being there. But I disagree. A restrained, well-mannered, quiet dog shouldn't be a problem. Predators at heart, dogs will cease every opportunity to chase the birds and animals of the forest. Please restrain your pet at all times to prevent mishaps. Those who do not want to leash their pet or keep it quiet should keep their dog at home.
7. Do not feed the wildlife. Leftover food may carry bacteria that is harmful to wildlife and animals can become dependent on humans for food.
8. Try to camp more than 100 feet from water and avoid camping in meadows, on top of flowers, and in wet places. Horses should be kept 200 feet from any water source.
9. Dispose of human waste properly. Using the cat method, dig a hole 6 to 8 inches deep, setting the top soil aside. After eliminating waste, cover up the hole, place top soil back on top, and if possible cover with a rock.
10. Wash your body, clothes, and dishes away from streams, spring, and lakes. Do not use any soap, including biodegradable, while standing in the water source. Move 100 feet away and wash there. And bury your toothpaste.

One special warning about drinking the water you will find rushing in rivers, cascading down rocky creeks, trickling down streams, and seeping up from natural springs. The water may contain organisms that cause glardiasis, also known as backpackers' diarrhea. Persons drinking from these water sources should boil the water before drinking or using in food preparation. Water purifiers and commercial water purification chemicals are also available.

The above suggestions are not intended to prevent someone from having a good time, but rather to insure a good time for our generation and the next and the next and all of those that follow. Now that the rules for wilderness travel are clear, you'll want to grab your pack and head for the hills. May God be with you during your many travels.

TIPS ON USING
THE BOOK, MAP, AND SO ON

MY GUIDE IS NOT YOUR TYPICAL HIKING GUIDE WITH DETAILED descriptions of various hikes throughout the state. Instead, it is a full-color guide mostly intended to give you a look at Oregon's vast and varied wilderness areas. In addition to color photographs, which will give you an idea of the places, the flora, and the fauna that you might well see, you'll find brief summaries of 100 hikes, some of the best in the state.

The wilderness areas are listed in alphabetical order and the hikes for each area are listed from one to 100. You can find a specific hike by looking at the map and finding the wilderness you most want to visit. You'll find numbers that correspond to each hike listed with each wilderness.

Because I've given just a brief summary of each hike, you'll want to make sure that you obtain and use the wilderness map listed with each hike. In addition to carrying a map, compass, and other necessities, always remember to carry water, food, bug repellent, and warm clothing just in case the weather changes. It can, and does, change quickly in the mountains so you'll always want to be prepared. Of course, you'll need additional supplies if you are backpacking instead of day hiking.

In addition to a portrait of each wilderness area, both a verbal one and a pictorial one, you'll find 100 hike descriptions. Each hike summary includes the length of the trail with mileage listed as either one-way or for the complete loop. I've rated the trails as easy to difficult, with easy being a short, fairly flat trail, moderate being a longer hike with some climbs, and difficult being a trek with some steep inclines.

It's tough to rate the trails, because what's moderate for me may be easy or difficult for you. Difficulty also depends on the weather, and a person's own attitude on a particular given day. So many things influence this rating; please keep that in mind when choosing a specific trail.

In addition to a description of the trail, I've included some trail highlights. Also I've denoted the high and low elevations (please remember

you may be climbing and descending between these two points), the best season for hiking, and I've listed the map that you should use for each trail. Also, I've included the address and phone number for the managing agency for each trail.

The listing for each hike also describes whether or not you will need some sort of permit to hike the trail of your choice. Many agencies ask that you fill out a self-issue hiking permit. These are available at the trailhead and help to keep track of the numbers of hikers who are visiting each area.

Many agencies are now participating in a new program, the "Trails for Generations" Trail Park Project. The new Trail-Park passes have been in effect in several Oregon Forests since July, 1997, and the number of agencies now requiring the pass is expanding. Hikers, horseback riders, and other recreation trail users are asked to pay parking fees at many trailheads. There's a fee of $3 per day or $25 for a year-long vehicle parking pass. The passes are good for all Oregon and Washington Forests.

According to the Forest Service, the "Trail-Park Pass is part of an experimental recreation fee program approved by Congress, who recognized the need to care for an aging and often overused national forest trail system where declining federal budgets could not keep pace with current trail use demands. At least 80 percent of the revenues will remain in the local areas where fees are collected to continue to offer high quality recreation opportunities."

In 1996, Congress authorized the Recreation Fee Demonstration Program for a three-year trial period. You may see changes in the regards to permits in the years to come. The plan is here for a while, however, so I would suggest checking beforehand to see if a trailhead that used to allow for free parking is now requiring a permit. Permits are available at Forest Service agencies, as well as some outdoor retail stores.

OREGON WILDERNESS AREAS

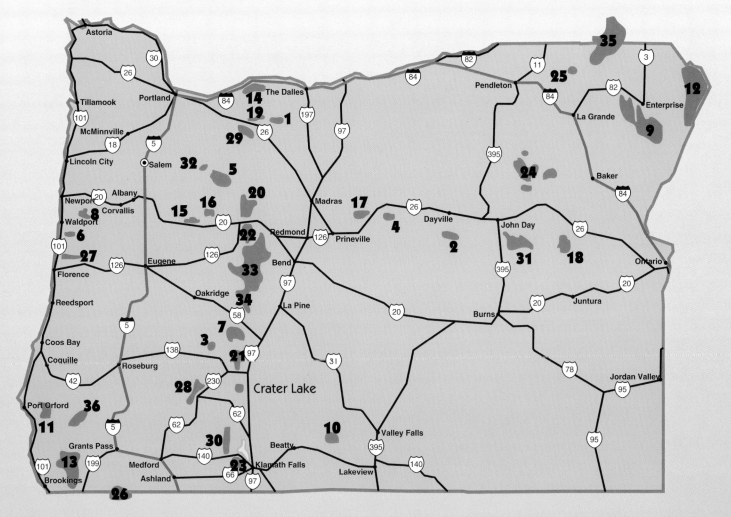

INTRODUCTION TO
THE BADGER CREEK WILDERNESS

Imagine a place where wildflowers dance along tiny creeks, swaying in the gentle breeze. Picture a place where wide vistas are yours for the asking. Visualize a place often uncrowded and lonely. Sound too good to be true? It might, but it's not for I found such a place in the Badger Creek Wilderness.

Although small in acreage, this 24,000 acre preserve is big on variety. Here, the High Cascades and Columbia Plateau Steppe greet one another with a mixture of forested canyons, steep slopes, talus slides, and basalt outcrops.

Located 65 miles southeast of Portland and 40 miles southwest of The Dalles, the preserve ranges in elevation from a low of 2,100 feet along Little Badger Creek to over 6,500 feet atop Lookout Mountain. A popular hike, from the summit of Lookout Mountain you'll see much of the Cascade Range (on a clear day see from Washington's Mt. Rainier to Oregon's Three Sisters) and the eastern high desert.

Three major drainages—Badger Creek, Little Badger Creek and Tygh Creek—slice through the diverse habitat. Here, hikers will find flora and fauna typical of both the west and east sides of the Cascades. Look for mountain hemlock, ponderosa pine, Oregon whiteoak, alpine rock gardens, and numerous grasses, shrubs, and wildflowers.

Two small lakes and 35-acre Badger Lake are located in the preserve. Badger Lake, the prime attraction and most popular site in the area, is part of an irrigation project, supplying water to private land to the east. A rough access road (no trailers permitted: high clearance vehicles recommended) leads to the 33-foot deep lake where fishermen hook rainbow and brook trout. Although the road leading to the lake is just outside the wilderness boundary, its trails and campsites are within the preserve.

The lower portion of Badger Creek (near Bonney Crossing Campground) is another well-liked fishing spot. Jean Lake is also a popular fishing lake, although most prefer fly fishing at the shallow, six-acre lake.

Whereas fishing is popular, hiking and horseback riding are the two most preferred uses.

Wildlife viewing is another rewarding pastime. This one, however, requires a bit of patience, but it's worth the effort.

Numerous animal species live in this protected environment. Designated wilderness in 1984, with the signing of the Oregon Wilderness Act (the preserve received prior protection upon designation as a Unroaded Recreation and Scenic Influence Zone in 1978), the area hosts 46 types of butterflies, and 157 species of birds, including wild turkeys, a prized game bird.

Attempts to transplant wild turkeys began in 1930, with the first successful transplantation taking place in 1961 when Merriam Turkeys were introduced from New Mexico and Arizona.

Mammals include elk, deer, and bear, all popular game species. Large mammals are often difficult to observe while hiking, but a patient hiker willing to sit quietly may see a species or two.

Oregonians know that if they are experiencing drippy weather on the west side of the Cascades, all they have to do is drive to the east and often they'll enjoy sunny, warm weather. Fortunately the 12-mile wide preserve rests on the east crest, where the annual precipitation ranges from 70 inches on the windy west-facing ridges to 20 inches in the dry eastern lowlands.

Snow usually closes the lower reaches in December and they usually remain closed through February. Given a relatively light winter snowpack, the highest trails are usually snowfree by mid- or late-June, with July, August, and September, the most popular months for visitors. In the summer, watch for afternoon thunderstorms.

Rocky Mountain elk (bull).

Badger.

BADGER CREEK (hike 1)

Trail length: About 11.1 miles one-way.
Description: Hike a portion of the trail for a day hike in the Badger Creek Wilderness; take two to three days and make it a nice back pack trip.
Difficulty: Moderate.
Highlights: Animal life; solitude; wildflowers; fishing.
Elevations: 4,472 to 2,200.
Maps: Badger Creek Wilderness Map.
Hiking season: June through November.
Permits: Trail Park Permit.
Contact: Barlow Ranger District, P.O. Box 67, Dufur, OR 97021; (541) 467-2291.
Directions: Two trailheads provide access to the trail. To reach the lowest end, drive a couple of miles beyond Bennett Pass, located on Oregon Highway 35, 32.2 miles south of Hood River. Go southeast on Forest Road 48, later traveling Forest Roads 4810, 4811, and 2710 for 22 miles to Bonney Crossing.

The west end of the trail (where this trail description begins) starts at the end of a bumpy road leading to Badger Lake Campground. Reach it by driving 32.2 miles south of the community of Hood River via Oregon Highway 35. At Bennett Pass, turn left on Forest Road 3550. This is a primitive road, not recommended for passenger cars; trailer use is not permitted.

Drive the gravel road for 1.8 miles to a fork; go left. After 3.4 miles make a right, traveling Forest Road 4860. In 2.1 miles come to another junction; make a left on Forest Road 140. Reach the Badger Lake Forest Camp after an additional 3.4 miles.
Trail info: Badger Creek Trail is a pleasant hike through the woods, with Badger Creek singing nearby. Wildflowers brighten up the forest: Look for crimson columbine, lilies, wild roses and strawberries, lupine and more.

Deer, elk and bear utilize the trails, toads hide under moist logs, graceful butterflies delight those who pass by. Woodpeckers, gros beaks, jays, and other birds flit from tree to tree.

It's a pleasant hike through a forest of Douglas-fir, hemlock, cedar, and ponderosa pines as you descend gradually (occasionally there's a moderate up and down), crossing many small streams along the way. Although you'll hear musical Badger Creek much of the time, you won't always be close enough to the creek to see it.

Vanilla leaf, trillium, huckleberries, and other plants adorn the forest floor as you hike this trail. Notice the vegetation change as you drop in elevation. Eventually you'll see oak trees and other low elevation plant life.

DIVIDE TRAIL (hike 2)

Trail length: About 4.3 miles one-way.
Description: A day hike in the Badger Creek Wilderness.
Difficulty: Moderate to strenuous.
Highlights: Grand vistas; wildflowers a plenty.
Elevations: 5,925 to 6,525 feet.
Maps: Badger Creek Wilderness Map.
Hiking season: July through October.
Permits: Trail Park Permit.
Contact: Barlow Ranger District, P.O. Box 67, Dufur, OR 97021; (541) 467-2291.
Directions: Drive south from Hood River via Oregon Highway 35 for 25.6 miles. At the Forest Road 44 exit (Dufur Mill Road), make a left and travel east for 3.8 miles to Forest Road 4410 (High Prairie Road); make a right, driving the gravel road for 4.7 miles to another junction. Head left on Forest Road 4420, an unmaintained road leading 0.1 mile east to the trailhead.

If you'd rather begin the hike at it's lowest point, you can begin hiking off Flag Point Lookout Road. Drive Forest Road 44 for 8.4 miles then head right on Forest Road 4420. In 2.1 miles the road forks; head straight on Forest Road 2730 towards the Flag Point Lookout. After 1.9 miles reach Forest Road 200, an unmaintained dirt road leading to the trailhead in about three miles.
Trail info: You'll find two trails at the High Prairie area, with a shorter one especially designed for the wheelchair-bound. Visit in July and you'll find a multitude of wildflowers—penstemon, Indian paint brush, avalanche lilies and a whole lot more—decorating the area. Along the ridge, look for "rock gardens" where wildflowers literally bloom from the rocks.

Reach a fork at 0.8 mile, going left to a junction at 1.2 miles. The Divide Trail 458 begins here. Keep left to reach Flag Point. Continue 100 yards to a junction; Lookout Summit is about 50 yards up the trail.

The view from atop the summit is spectacular. Highlights include Washington's Mounts St. Helens, Adams, and Rainier. Oregon offers Mount Hood and Mount Jefferson, as well as The Three Sisters, Broken Top, and the Columbia River drainage.

Go back to the junction and descend a steep grade to another junction at 1.4 miles. Alternate between forest and open ridge until reaching the Fret Creek Trail junction at 2.8 miles. Now it's a steep climb back up to the ridgetop and some very interesting rock formations. Climb and then descend again as you make your way to the trailhead.

Kelly's tiger lily.

13

INTRODUCTION TO THE BLACK CANYON WILDERNESS

Steep canyons, sharp ridges, tree-covered mesas, wildflowers, and an abundance of wildlife can all be found in Black Canyon Wilderness. Solitude can also be enjoyed by those who visit in the spring and summer season, before hunters flock to the area in the fall.

Black Canyon Wilderness is located near the heart of Oregon, 57 miles east of Prineville, and 35 miles west of John Day. Comprised of 13,400 acres, the area was designated as such by Congress with the passage of the Oregon Wilderness Act of 1984.

Managed exclusively by the Ochoco National Forest, the area was first considered for wilderness classification for several reasons. First, it met the criteria for remoteness, solitude and size. In addition, Black Canyon is a watershed which has had little direct human-caused impacts. Also, it is representative of a variety of Central Oregon vegetation types.

Black Canyon Creek drains through the wilderness from the west to the east, dropping over 3,000 feet in the process. As it nears its low point in the east, Black Canyon Creek flows into the South Fork of the John Day River. Anglers should note that the best fishing occurs early in the season for Black Canyon Creek is a fairly small stream. The fish tend to be small as well.

Seventeen miles of trails traverse the wilderness. Elevation varies with the lowest point of 2,850 feet located at the eastern boundary where Black Canyon Creek joins the South Fork of the John Day River on Bureau of Land Management land. The highest point, 6,483 feet, is located near Wolf Mountain Lookout. Located a few hundred feet outside the wilderness, the lookout provides a great view and is currently manned each summer.

A wide range in elevation provides a variety of terrain to explore. Volcanic ash soils cover about one-third of the area with nearly one-half of the wilderness devoid of trees. Most of these non-timbered openings are located on ridge tops or south facing slopes. Northern slopes generally support a forest of mixed conifers, and southern slopes usually contain a mixture of ponderosa pine, juniper, and mixed conifers. Over fifty percent of the timbered sections are considered old-growth forest.

Snow and cold temperatures invade the area each winter, but the area is usually snowfree around June and normally remains open until the beginning of November. Temperatures vary in this part of Oregon, with daytime summer highs ranging from the low 40's to the high 90's. Nighttime lows, during the summer months, usually dip to anywhere between 30 and 60 degrees. Winter temperatures range from the teen's to the 40's during the day with nights 20 to 40 degrees colder.

Wildlife and wildflowers abound although flowers are much more easily observed. Wild animals tend to be very shy, but still it is exciting just knowing they are there. Three hundred species of wildlife are common to the Ochoco National Forest, most of which may exist in the wilderness. Common big game species include elk and deer. Also, there may be the chance to see the rarely-observed mountain lion which is believed to inhabit the area as well. Other species include, black bear, coyotes, marmots, porcupines, and badgers. Of course, the bird life found here is equally exciting.

Rattlesnakes are one species of animal life that hikers should be aware of. Mosquitoes do not appear to be a problem.

A variety of wildflowers paint the area during the early summer months. The Forest Service recommends viewing wildflowers before July, as Central Oregon's hot dry days and fairly cool nights force flowers to bloom just after snowmelt.

BLACK CANYON (hike 3)

Trail length: About 11.6 miles one-way.
Description: Hike a portion of the trail for a day hike or make it a back pack trip into the Black Canyon Wilderness.
Difficulty: Moderate to strenuous.
Highlights: Old-growth forest; beautiful creek; fishing; solitude; wild flowers and wildlife. Watch for rattlesnakes.

Elevations: 6,400 to 2,850.
Maps: Wolf Mountain, Aldrich Gulch 7.5-minute USGS quads.
Hiking season: June through November.
Permits: None required; limit group size to 12 people/stock.
Contact: Paulina Ranger District, 171500 Beaver Creek Rd., Paulina, OR 97751; (541) 477-3713.
Directions: From Prineville, drive 63 miles east via U.S. Highway 26, then turn right (south) on Forest Road 12. Travel 15.6 miles then make a left on Forest Road 1250; go another 3.9 miles. At the junction head straight, now driving Forest Road 090; stay on it for 3.6 miles. The road may be rocky, but in good weather it is usually passable for passenger cars. Make a left on Forest Road 5820; continue another 0.4 mile to Forest Road 5840. Drive this 2.5 miles to the trailhead.
Trail info: Black Canyon Trail traverses an old-growth forest of Douglas-fir and ponderosa pine, and allows one to enjoy Black Canyon Creek. Hikers must ford Owl Creek once and Black Canyon Creek 20 times. Also, there are numerous other small stream crossings.

Besides scenic value, the area also offers the chance to observe animal life and a variety of wildflowers—look for columbine, ladys-slipper, lupine, and paintbrush during the late spring/early summer.

Hike Black Canyon Trail 820 by descending through the trees or semi-open slope to Owl Creek at 3.0 miles. Cross Owl Creek then descend moderately to Black Canyon Creek at 3.2 miles.

At 9.4 miles cross Payten Creek. Now you'll begin a series of 14 creek crossings in the next two miles. Reach the South Fork John Day River at 11.6 miles. Those with a shuttle available can ford the South Fork John Day River and have a car waiting on South Fork Road, located on Bureau of Land Management land.

Please note, in addition to seeing mammals and birds, you may also observe rattlesnakes. Use caution!

Facing page: Black Canyon Creek, Black Canyon Wilderness.
Below: Broadleaf lupine.

Introduction To
The Boulder Creek Wilderness

Steep and rugged, the Boulder Creek Wilderness is rich in old-growth forest, numerous rock monoliths, small streams, and plant and animal life. Boulder Creek, a tributary of the North Umpqua River, flows through the middle of the wilderness, its waters an important spawning stream for anadromous fish. Small waterfalls, rushing rapids, and tiny, quiet pools of water, combine to make Boulder Creek a nice spot to visit.

Designated wilderness on June 26, 1984, Boulder Creek Wilderness is located on the west side of the Cascade Mountains, 50 miles east of Roseburg, Oregon. The 19,100-acre preserve is located in and managed by the Umpqua National Forest. The wilderness ranges in elevation from a low of 1,600 feet near the southern boundary to a high of 5,600 feet near the northern wilderness boundary.

There are some interesting geologic areas to visit in the southern portion. At Pine Bench you'll find a 140-acre stand of old growth ponderosa pine, a rarity for an area this far north and west of the summit of the Cascades.

Also of interest is the Umpqua Rocks Geological Area, an area comprised of spires of basalt and interesting cliffs, located partially within the southern portion of the wilderness.

For those who would like to fish in Boulder Creek please note that state regulations require fly fishing only. There are rainbow and cutthroat trout in the creek, but they are usually small and hardly worth keeping.

There are plenty of wildflowers for everyone to enjoy during the spring and early summer months. See, smell, and touch these beautiful wonders of nature, but please don't pick them. Give others the chance to enjoy the beauty of each delicate wildflower.

Boreal toad.

Wildlife lovers will be thrilled to know there are black bear and mountain lions roaming the area. Of course, these two species are rarely encountered, but there is always a thrill in just knowing they are there. In addition, you may also find deer, elk, spotted owl and many other species.

An unwelcome critter—the mosquito—appears in the spring after snow melt. There are quite a few of the pests at this time of year, but there are less mosquitoes here than at higher elevations.

Portions of the wilderness are generally accessible year-round. Those areas below 2500 feet are usually free of snow, but the higher elevations receive an average of four to five feet of snow. The area is usually snow-free from mid-June to early November. Spring and fall are the best times to visit the wilderness as temperatures can be quite hot in the summer.

BOULDER CREEK (hike 4)

Trail length: About 10.3 miles one-way.
Description: A day hike (with shuttle access) or an overnight backpack in the Boulder Creek Wilderness.
Difficulty: Moderate to strenuous.
Highlights: Old-growth forest and an abundance of solitude.
Elevations: 2,200 to 5,300 feet.
Maps: Boulder Creek Wilderness Map.
Hiking season: Mid-June through early November.
Permits: None required; limit group size to 12 people/stock.
Contact: Diamond Lake Ranger District, 2020 Toketee Ranger Station Road, Idleyld Park, OR 97447; (541) 498-2531.
Directions: The Soda Springs Trailhead is located a couple of miles west of Tokatee off Oregon Highway 138. At the "Soda Spring Reservoir" sign head north, immediately making a left on the dirt road. Follow this road past the dam and park at the Soda Springs Trailhead, 1.3 miles from Highway 138.

To reach Bear Camp Trailhead, the northernmost and highest of the two trailheads, drive to the junction of Oregon Highway 138 and Forest Road 38 at Steamboat. Head northeast on Road 38 for 11 miles; turn right on Road 3817 and continue on this for 3 miles to Forest Road 3850. Head down Road 3850 for 8 miles. (Road 3850 turns into Road 3810 at this point). Continue along Road 3810 for 1.5 miles to the signed trailhead.
Trail info: Boulder Creek Trail traverses the length of the wilderness from north-to-south, sometimes paralleling the creek and sometimes not.

From the Bear Camp Trailhead, begin descending (and occasionally ascending) Boulder Creek Trail 1552, reaching Boulder Creek after 3.3 miles. Cross from one side of the creek to the other as the trail continues to descend.

At 5.0 miles head away from the creek, reaching Spring Mountain Trail at 5.9 miles. Stay straight, continuing to the junction of Onion Creek and Boulder Creek at 6.3 miles.

Waterfall in the Boulder Creek Wilderness.

As you leave the creek again, climb, descend, and climb to 7.2 miles and the junction of Perry Butte Trail. As you hike notice the large stand of Ponderosa Pine trees. Known as Pine Bench, this 140-acre stand of Ponderosas is believed to be the largest stand this far north and west of the summit of the Cascade Mountains.

At 8.3 miles reach the junction of the Boulder Creek and Bradley Trails. Turn left onto Bradley Trail 1491, descending to Soda Stub Trail at 9.8 miles. Take the Soda Stub Trail to the right and descend to the trailhead at 10.3 miles.

INTRODUCTION TO
THE BRIDGE CREEK WILDERNESS

Of Oregon's 36 designated wilderness areas, Bridge Creek Wilderness has the distinction of being the third smallest. Steep terrain, open meadows, forested slopes, and scab flats, also known as plateaus, in addition to solitude and great views, combine to make this area a nice place to visit.

Bridge Creek was designated a wilderness in 1984 when the Oregon Wilderness Act was signed by President Reagan. Chosen for it's excellent wildlife habitat, 5,400-acre Bridge Creek is located 30 miles east/north-east of Prineville.

A 3.5-mile trail penetrates the preserve but the trail is not maintained and there are no plans to upgrade it. Also, there is an old road which leads one mile to North Point and a spectacular view. The Forest Service has chosen to manage the area as a trailless wilderness. The area ranges in elevation from 4,360 feet at the northern boundary to 6,607 feet at the southern boundary near Carroll Camp.

A mixed conifer forest of white fir, Douglas-fir, western larch, and some lodgepole pine and ponderosa pine cover about four-fifths of the area with one-fifth of the wilderness being open. In addition, there are sagebrush, snowberry, and other brush species.

There are 5.8 miles of streams with Bridge Creek flowing through the center of the preserve in a south to north direction. At one time Bridge Creek was a water source for the small community of Mitchell, located to the north. Today, however, the community depends on wells and springs instead of Bridge Creek. Other water sources in the area include Maxwell Creek and five springs: Thompson, Pisgah, Masterson, Nelson, and Maxwell.

Hikers will find July, August, September, and October, the best times for visiting. Snow makes access difficult during late fall, winter, and early spring.

Bridge Creek is rarely crowded, but in the fall it becomes a popular hunting area. An excellent elk wintering area, the Wilderness is used by some elk throughout the year. Other large mammals found in the area include mule deer, bear and mountain lion.

Several unique species of bird life may also be seen as pileated woodpeckers, goshawks, and prairie falcons nest within the wilderness. To date, there have been no sightings of any endangered species.

Blue grouse.

Mountain lion.

NORTH POINT TRAIL (hike 5)

Trail length: About 1.0 mile one-way.
Description: A short day hike in the Bridge Creek Wilderness.
Difficulty: Easy.
Highlights: Nice view.
Elevations: 6,200 to 6,540 feet.
Maps: Mt. Pisgah USGS quad.
Hiking season: July through October.
Permits: None required.
Contact: Big Summit Ranger District, HC 69, Box 255,
   Prineville, OR 97754.
Directions: To reach the trailhead drive 17 miles east on U.S. Highway 26 from the junction of Highways 26 and 126 in Prineville. Turn right on the paved road (sign states: "Ochoco R.S.") and follow this for 8.7 miles; make a left on Forest Road 22, driving past Walton Lake and continuing to the end of pavement at 8.1 miles.
   Head to the left, now driving Forest Road 150. Curve to the right at 0.8 mile now traveling on Forest Road 2630. Reach Thompson Spring 3.7 miles farther and a sign for Bridge Creek Wilderness. Continue straight and reach Bridge Creek and an old road (trailhead) at 2.0 miles. Carroll Camp and Pisgah Spring is located 0.2 mile down the road.
Trail info: This trail isn't really a trail: Instead, it's an old road that at one time lead to a lookout at North Point. Although the lookout was replaced with the one visible to the south on Mt. Pisgah, the view remains fantastic from this easy-to-reach site.
   The trail starts near Carroll Camp, a primitive camp. The first portion of the trail leads across meadows, along Bridge Creek, then up across an open ridge where there is a nice view. Later the trail heads down into the trees, crossing two springs before ending at the northern boundary of the wilderness.
   Begin hiking the road, heading north for the 1.0 mile trek to North Point. The road is lined with thick pines, good habitat for the grouse I observed while hiking this trail. From North Point the view is terrific with the Cascade Range visible to the west. Portions of Bridge Creek Wilderness and other points can be viewed as well.

Mule deer (buck).

Protection for this beautiful region came about in 1969. Designated a scenic area at that time, it later became a National Forest Wilderness with passage of the Oregon Wilderness Bill in 1984.

Elevations in the region range from 2,000 feet to 5,700 feet with many of the lower slopes covered with dense stands of timber. Slopes are usually steep with grades of 30 to 60 percent. The upper slopes are even steeper, with inclines of 60 to 90 percent. Most of these are covered by dense timber as well.

As mentioned previously, crowds are few in this subalpine region. Opting for more popular areas, most pass Bull of the Woods by to hike in other areas covered in this guide. But this area has plenty to offer. There are a dozen or so fish-bearing lakes, surrounded by high ridges. Several rivers—the Collawash, Breitenbush, and Little North Fork Santiam—dissect the region.

Bird life is plentiful. Five owl species make the Bull of the Woods Wilderness their home. Look for the controversial northern spotted owl, a beautiful bird imperiled by loss of its old-growth habitat. Other silent creatures-of-the-night include, the great horned owl, screech owl, pygmy owl, and the tiny saw-whet owl.

In addition to the bird life, there are a variety of mammals in the region. Most commonly seen are deer, with elk being sighted on occasion. Although the area does receive some hunting use, it isn't a favorite haunt as early snows usually move animals out of the region before hunting season gets under way.

Prospectors once flocked to the area, but not to see the animal life. They were looking for a big strike—the kind that can make one as rich as a king. Look for abandoned mines throughout the area, and you'll see some small mines (containing scanty amounts of copper and silver) here and there along Battle Ax Creek at Jawbone Flats as well. Watch for mine shafts, old pieces of equipment, and other man-made features.

INTRODUCTION TO THE BULL OF THE WOODS WILDERNESS

Some know it as the "Hidden Wilderness," others think of it whenever the words "steep terrain" are mentioned, and still others remember its flowery meadows. When I sit and recollect I recall vast old-growth forests, rugged ridges, endless vistas, quiet pools, a waterfall, and beavers cruising a glassy lake. Often I dream of the Bull of the Woods Wilderness.

Managed by both the Mt. Hood and Willamette National Forests, the 34,900-acre preserve rests 68 miles southeast of Portland and 65 miles east of Salem.

Average in size, this wilderness provides "opportunities for solitude," one of the objectives of the Wilderness Act. Here, in the middle of the week, it is still possible to hike all day and not encounter another party. Several trails receive heavy use, however, and should be avoided by those wanting a more pristine experience.

One such busy place is the Bull of the Woods Lookout whereby hikers can stand on the 5,523-foot summit and see from Washington's Mt. Rainier to Oregon's Mt. Hood, Mt. Jefferson, the Three Sisters and beyond.

Hikers encounter 75 miles of trail (most maintained annually) leading through dense old-growth forest, and steep, mountainous terrain. Also there's the chance for exquisite vistas from several small peaks.

Speaking of old-growth, Bull of the Woods is one of the last great old-growth reserves in western Oregon. Western hemlock, Douglas-fir, and Pacific Silver fir are present with a multitude of lichens, mosses, and other life visible. Those interested in flowers will find plenty to keep them busy. Look for white trillium and Oregon grape blossoms in the deep forest in April; early July brings a confusion of rhododendrons, delighting all who visit.

Welcome Creek, Bull of the Woods Wilderness.

18

ELK LAKE CREEK (hike 6)

Trail length: About 9.2 miles one-way.

Description: A long day hike or an overnight backpack trip into the Bull of the Woods Wilderness.

Difficulty: Moderate.

Highlights: Old-growth forest; fishing; solitude.

Elevations: 3,900 to 2,500 feet.

Maps: Bull of the Woods Wilderness Map.

Hiking season: Mid-June through October.

Permits: Trail Park Permit.

Contact: Estacada Ranger District, 595 NW Industrial Way, Estacada, OR 97023; (503) 630-4256.

Directions: You can begin hiking from two trailheads. This hike starts at the Elk Lake Trailhead near Elk Lake, but you can also begin hiking from a trailhead off Forest Road 6380. (See MOTHER LODE LOOP for more information.)

From the small town of Detroit, where you'll find the junction of Oregon Highway 22 and paved Forest Road 46, head northeast on Road 46. At 4.3 miles turn left on paved Forest Road 4696. Make another left on gravel Forest Road 4697 in 0.8 mile. After 4.6 miles a sign warns that the road is now a "Rough Road." The Forest Service recommends high clearance vehicles for the last 1.5 miles to the trail head.

Park where Elk Lake Creek flows from Elk Lake. The trail begins a short distance up the road, but there isn't room for parking.

Trail info: Hike down the road 0.1 mile to unsigned Elk Lake Creek Trail 559. Turn right and begin hiking through beautiful old-growth forest.

Cross several small streams and springs before reaching Battle Creek Shelter and a junction at 4.1 miles. Continue straight, fording Battle Creek at 4.4 miles.

Reach Elk Lake Creek at 5.5 miles; ford the creek, now traveling the east side. Soon after, the trail enters a very scenic gorge with towering cliffs, beautiful little pools, and the emerald-like waters of Elk Lake Creek cascading down, eventually flowing into the East Fork Collawash River at a point near the northern trailhead.

At 6.8 miles you'll have to ford Elk Lake Creek again. After this

Wilderness Mushrooms.

Spotted owl.

crossing the trail remains on the west side of the creek. Please note: Use caution when crossing as creek waters can be deep and swift.

Reach the unmarked junction to Welcome Lakes at 6.9 miles. Ford Pine Cone Creek at 8.4 miles and exit the wilderness soon after. At 8.7 miles reach a pretty waterfall and your last look at Elk Lake Creek. From here, continue to the trailhead off Road 6380 at 9.2 miles.

MOTHER LODE LOOP (hike 7)

Trail length: About 19.0 miles for the complete loop.

Description: A backpack trip in the Bull of the Woods Wilderness or a day hike if you hike the first few miles.

Difficulty: Strenuous, though the first few miles are easy.

Highlights: Waterfall; old-growth forest; fishing; abundant animal life; grand view from Bull of the Woods Lookout.

Elevations: 2,500 to 5,523 feet.

Maps: Bull of the Woods Wilderness Map.

Hiking season: Mid-June through October.

Permits: Trail Park Permit.

Contact: Estacada Ranger District, 595 NW Industrial Way, Estacada, OR 97023; (503) 630-4256.

Directions: To reach the trailhead at Elk Lake Creek drive to Detroit, where you'll find the junction of U.S. Highway 22 and Forest Road 46. Head northeast on paved Highway 46; after 4.3 miles turn left on Forest Road 4697. Go 2.2 miles and turn right on Forest Road 4698, a gravel road which later turns to Road 6370.

You'll pass acres of clearcuts as you continue another 18.9 miles to a junction. Make a left, now traveling Forest Road 6380. Reach the trailhead in 2.8 miles.

Trail info: Begin hiking Elk Lake Trail 559, passing a waterfall and fording the creek and other streams on occasion. Most are easy to cross, but you should always use caution as waters can be deep and swift.

At 2.3 miles reach an unmarked trail to Welcome Lakes. This will be your return trail. Continue up the creek, entering a very scenic gorge with towering cliffs, deep pools, and the most beautiful emerald-like water imaginable. Reach the collapsed Battle Ax Shelter at 5.1 miles. Now travel northwest on the Mother Lode Trail 558, crossing Mother Lode Creek and hiking on to 7.5 miles and the turnoff for Twin Lakes. (It's less than 3 miles each way to the lakes.)

Reach Bull of the Woods Trail 550 and access to the Bull of the Woods Lookout at 11.2 miles. Travel north, climbing to the lookout in 0.6 mile. The view is outstanding from the summit. Washington's major peaks include Mounts Saint Helens, Rainier, and Adams. Oregon's highlights include Mounts Hood and Jefferson, as well as the Three Sisters.

Back at the junction head left on Welcome Lakes Trail 554. At 16.7 miles reach the junction of Elk Creek Lake Trail; go left, heading back the way you came in.

INTRODUCTION TO THE CUMMINS CREEK WILDERNESS

Dense rain forest and solitude combine to make the Cummins Creek Wilderness a special place to visit. See some of the finest examples of Sitka spruce trees, and enjoy a day of peace and quiet. Be prepared, however, to hike along an old road, as maintained trails are nonexistent and the thick vegetation makes cross-country travel nearly impossible.

This region is often difficult to explore for dense undergrowth prevails. Look for light pink rhododendron blooms in May. Other plant species include salal, sword fern and salmonberry. Watch for red alder, bigleaf maple, and vine maple lining the creeks. Wildflowers (including yellow monkeyflowers, purple asters and delicate candyflowers) often enchant spring visitors. In addition, there are red foxglove and lily-of-the-valley.

Ringed by roads, the 26-square-mile preserve lies about 15 miles north of Florence and 5 miles south of Waldport. Established in 1984 with the signing of the Oregon Wilderness Act, the 9,173-acre preserve is managed by the Siuslaw National Forest.

The Forest Service allows hikers into the area but it does not allow horses: The fragile soil is not compatible with horse travel.

Elevation ranges from 100 feet near the Pacific Ocean to 2400 feet close to Cummins Peak. Two principal streams—Cummins Creek and Bob Creek—drain into the Pacific. Both support significant runs of anadromous fish.

Western trillium.

Anglers should note that the Forest Service claims the fishing isn't very good in Cummins Creek, but it is a good spawning area.

Sixty to eighty inches of rain fall upon this land of steep valleys, Sitka spruce, hemlock, and Douglas-fir. In the summer, chilly fogs envelop the coast and nearby valleys. Winters are usually free of snow. While year-round access is possible, fall and spring are the best times to visit for there's a better chance of clear skies.

Wildlife abounds in the region. The controversial spotted owl nests here as well as other owl and bird species. Animal making their home here include Roosevelt elk, black-tailed deer and black bear.

Two trails begin at the Cummins Ridge Trailhead. The only wilderness trail (the first 3.5-miles of which consist of an abandoned road) continues east from the trailhead, traveling 6.2 miles along the ridgetop. An unofficial trail heads north from the barricade, just outside the wilderness boundary. The unmaintained spur road is not suitable for vehicles. Keep left on this spur for less than a half mile to a scenic bench of old-growth Sitka spruce.

CUMMINS RIDGE (hike 8)

Trail length: About 6.2 miles one-way.

Description: A day hike in the Cummins Creek Wilderness.

Difficulty: Moderate.

Highlights: Dense Sitka spruce and Douglas-fir stands; solitude and quiet.

Elevations: 880 to 2,040 feet.

Maps: Cummins Creek Wilderness Map.

Hiking season: Year-round.

Permits: Trail Park Permit.

Contact: Waldport Ranger District, P.O. Box 400, Waldport, OR 97394; (541) 563-3211.

Directions: To reach the trailhead, drive 4.6 miles south from Yachats via U.S. Highway 101. From the main highway, turn east onto Forest Road 1051 and drive 2.2 miles to the trailhead.

Trail info: Cummins Creek Wilderness is a place where getting around isn't easy. The vegetation is nearly impenetrable; it's steep and rugged and hikers prefer using trails whenever possible.

The Cummins Ridge Trail consists of an old logging road for the first 3.5 miles, the remaining 2.7 miles of which are trail. The road is covered with grass and other vegetation, making a slow comeback to what was once dense vegetation. As you hike, notice the sweet smells of the forest, listen for birds singing, and look for elk and bear scat of which I saw plenty.

The trail heads up at a moderate grade then descends some before reaching the end of the road at 2.9 miles. Before the trail ends, look for a trail leading off to the left. For a good view of the wilderness, take this trail for several hundred yards and you'll see the Pacific, and other points north of here.

Vine maple in the fall.

INTRODUCTION TO
THE DIAMOND PEAK WILDERNESS

Common goldeneye (drake).

Wildflowers dance in the wind. Elk bugle during the fall rut. Deer tiptoe quietly through dense forests. Marmots chase each other over boulder fields, their antics like children playing. Clear mountain streams crisscross the land. Deep blue lakes dot the landscape. Formed by angry volcanic activity, many of the lakes fill depressions, scratched out of the surface by mighty glaciers. And above it all stands the guardian of the wilderness—Diamond Peak.

Located in the Cascade Mountains of central Oregon, the 8,744-foot peak is one of hundreds of old volcanoes that make up the expansive "Ring of Fire." At one time the mountain reached hundreds of feet higher into the heavens, but glaciers cut deeply into the immense mountain, gorging out glacial cirques, chopping Diamond Peak down to its present size.

On February 5, 1957 the Forest Service established the 36,637-acre Diamond Peak Wild Area. In 1964, it was reclassified wilderness by the Wilderness Act. Later, with passage of the Oregon Wilderness Act of 1984, the wilderness increased to its present size—54,185 acres.

Diamond Peak is the area's most prominent peak, with two other tall peaks—Mt. Yoran and Lakeview Mountain—reaching high into the heavens as well. Climbers bag summits on all three peaks. The most popular route to Diamond Peak's lofty summit is from the south ridge. Although not a difficult climb, one should never attempt to reach the summit alone.

Mt. Yoran, at 7,138 feet, offers skilled mountaineers the chance to scale a steep precipice. Experienced climbers scale Lakeview Mountain as well.

Both the Willamette and Deschutes National Forests manage the wilderness: The Willamette cares for 19,772 acres of preserve, the Deschutes 34,413 acres. Approximately 125 miles of trails exist in the wilderness, which ranges in elevation from 4,787 feet near Odell Lake to a high of 8,744 feet atop Diamond Peak. The Pacific Crest National Scenic Trail (PCNST) divides the area, skirting the east slope of Diamond Peak from north to south.

While today's visitors come to hike, relax, fish, and photograph, a century ago folks came for other reasons. For example, the members of the "Lost Wagon Train" came searching for the Willamette Valley. En route from Allegheny City, Pennsylvania, during October of 1853, the pioneers hoped to find a primitive road leading over the mountains to the fertile valley. They found none.

With winter just around the corner, the wagon train members were desperate to reach the other side of the mountain. On they pushed, up through the mountains, carving a rough road in the harsh landscape. Hardy folks that they were, they inched forward, probably guided by the snow-covered slopes of Diamond Peak. (John Diamond scaled the peak the previous year in an attempt to look for a pass through the mountains. The peak was named for him.) West of the summit, the pioneers were nearly heartbroken as they viewed a sea of timber stretching out before them. Too close to give up, they sent out one of their men for help. A rescue party from the valley met the 1,500 starving pioneers and everyone reached safety and the town of Butte Disappointment (known as Lowell today).

Although distraught at the time, the pioneers undoubtedly realized that the area was rich in timber and other vegetation. Douglas-fir and western hemlock blanket most of Diamond Peak's west side. True fir,

Backpackers and samoyed in the Diamond Peak Wilderness.

Beargrass plume.

turn right on Forest Road 2160. Drive 4.1 miles on this road until you reach Forest Road 2149 and a sign "Bear Mountain." Head to the right and continue 4.9 miles to the trailhead.

Trail info: Hike Blue Lake Trail 3645 through the trees, gradually ascending to Blue Lake at 0.6 mile. To continue to Happy Lake, keep to the left, crossing over a creek at and reaching the north end Blue Lake at 0.9 mile. The trail turns abruptly at this point, heading up a ridge via switchback. Although unsigned, the trail is easy to follow if you look for blazed trees and cut logs. Reach Diamond Peak Trail 3699 at 1.7 miles.

Head to the left, crossing two streams en route to the junction of Happy Lake at 2.7 miles. Turn left on Happy Lake Trail 3653 and descend moderately to lake.

CORRIGAN LAKE (hike 10)

Trail length: About 1.4 miles one-way.
Description: A day hike in the Diamond Peak Wilderness.
Difficulty: Easy.
Highlights: Fishing; nice view of Diamond Peak.
Elevations: 4,960 to 5,600 feet.
Maps: Diamond Peak Wilderness Map.
Hiking season: July through October.
Permits: Wilderness Permit; Trail Park Permit.
Contact: Rigdon Ranger Station, P.O. Box 1410, Oakridge, OR 97463; (541) 782-2283.
Directions: To reach the trailhead drive 35 miles southeast of Oakridge via Oregon Highway 58 to the small town of Crescent Lake. Head southwest on paved Crescent Lake Road and reach a junction of Forest Road 60 at 2.3 miles. Turn right at the sign: "Summit Lake -

Red-breasted sapsucker (male).

mountain hemlock and western white pine cover much of the remaining area. And dense stands of lodgepole pines cover the eastern half. Thick understory carpets much of the ground in the true fir-hemlock forest. Huckleberries and dwarf manzanita are the most common.

There are many species of wildflowers such as lupine, trillium, penstemon, Indian paint brush, shooting stars, rhododendrons, and more. Wildlife is abundant as well. Mammals include black-tailed deer and elk, bear, and small mammals such as marmots, snowshoe rabbits, pine martens, foxes, squirrels, and pika inhabit the area all year long.

There are many species of bird life too. Most common are the dipper or water ouzel, and the grouse. Other species include Clark's nutcracker, gray jay, Oregon junco, and raven. Bufflehead, goldeneye, and wood ducks nest near some of the lakes.

BLUE AND HAPPY LAKES (hike 9)

Trail length: About 3.2 miles one-way.
Description: A day hike in the Diamond Peak Wilderness.
Difficulty: Easy to moderate.
Highlights: Wildflowers; great scenes; fishing.
Elevations: 5,600 to 5,920 feet.
Maps: Diamond Peak Wilderness Map.
Hiking season: July through October.
Permits: Wilderness Permit; Trail Park Permit.
Contact: Rigdon Ranger Station, P.O. Box 1410, Oakridge, OR 97463; (541) 782-2283.
Directions: To reach the trailhead travel 35 miles southeast of Oakridge via Oregon Highway 58 to the town of Crescent Lake. Head south west on paved Crescent Lake Road and reach a junction of Forest Road 60 at 2.3 miles. Turn right at the sign: "Summit Lake - 12 miles." Drive the paved road along the north end of Crescent Lake to the junction of Forest Road 6010, another 5.1 miles down the road.

Turn right onto Road 6010, traveling the unmaintained dirt road (passenger cars okay) to Emigrant Pass, another 6.6 miles away. Summit Lake and campground are to your left as you head right on Forest Road 380.

Continue traveling the dirt road for another mile or so then the road turns to a good gravel road. At 2.3 miles from Emigrant Pass

Gray fox.

12 miles." Drive the paved road along the north end of Crescent Lake to the junction of Forest Road 6010, another 5.1 miles down the road.

Turn right onto Road 6010, traveling the unmaintained dirt road (passenger cars okay) to Emigrant Pass, another 6.6 miles away. Summit Lake and campground are to your left as you head right on Forest Road 380.

Continue for another mile or so then the road turns to a good gravel road. At 2.3 miles from Emigrant Pass turn right on Forest Road 2160. Drive 4.1 miles on this road until you reach Forest Road 2149 and a sign "Bear Mountain." Head to the right and continue to the trailhead at 1.2 miles.

Trail info: Corrigan Lake Trail 3654 leads through the trees, roaming amidst a lush alpine forest of mountain hemlock and grand, silver, and noble fir.

Switchback and wind you way up to a junction at 1.4 miles. Diamond Peak Trail is straight ahead. Head to the right and towards Corrigan Lake, 100 yards away.

Diamond Peak provides a splendid backdrop for Corrigan Lake when viewed from the west. Fishermen will find the fishing equally splendid, with brook trout hooked quite often.

DIAMOND VIEW LAKE/DIAMOND PEAK LOOP
(hike 11)

Trail length: About 23.3 miles for the complete loop.
Description: A backpack trip in the Diamond Peak Wilderness.
Difficulty: Moderate to strenuous.
Highlights: Wide vistas; scenic lakes; wildlife; fishing.
Elevations: 4,800 to 7,040 feet.
Maps: Diamond Peak Wilderness Map.
Hiking season: July through October.
Permits: Wilderness Permit; Trail Park Permit.
Contact: Rigdon Ranger Station, P.O. Box 1410, Oakridge, OR 97463; (541) 782-2283, or Crescent Ranger District, P.O. Box 208, Crescent, OR 97733; (541) 433-2234.
Directions: The loop begins at West Odell Campground at Odell Lake. It is 28 miles southeast of Oakridge, via Oregon Highway. 58. Turn right at the signed junction and descend Forest Road 5810 (Odell Lake Rd.), reaching the trailhead for Mount Yoran Lake at 1.8 miles.
Trail info: Begin hiking Mount Yoran Trail 49 by crossing the railroad tracks then climbing gradually to a junction at 0.2 mile. To the right lies the Willamette Pass; Mount Yoran lies straight ahead. To begin the loop, head left on Whitefish Creek Trail 42 to Crescent Lake. Reach Diamond View Lake—where you'll have a terrific view of the 8,744-foot extinct volcano—at 5.0 miles.

Reach another junction at 5.8 miles; head right on Crater Butte Trail 44 which leads to the Pacific Crest Trail (PCT) at 10.5 miles; make a right, now hiking north on the PCT. At 11.7 miles there's a fantastic view of Summit Lake to the south and numerous Cascade

peaks. This point is also the jumping off point for those hiking up the south spur to the top of Diamond Peak.

Reach a spur trail leading to Midnight Lake at 21.3 miles. Continue to a junction at 21.5 miles where a blue sign points straight to Gold Lake Snow Park, 2.7 miles away.

Head straight from this point and reach the wilderness boundary at 22.5 miles. Turn left on an old road and go 200 feet to another blue signed junction. Turn right to reach Odell Lake Road, completing the loop at 23.3 miles.

DIVIDE LAKE (hike 12)

Trail length: About 4.0 miles one-way.
Description: A day hike in the Diamond Peak Wilderness.
Difficulty: Moderate.
Highlights: Good views of Diamond Peak and numerous other peaks; old-growth forest; fishing.
Elevations: 5,280 to 6,400 feet.
Maps: Diamond Peak Wilderness Map.
Hiking season: July through October.
Permits: Wilderness Permit; Trail Park Permit.
Contact: Rigdon Ranger Station, P.O. Box 1410, Oakridge, OR 97463; (541) 782-2283.
Directions: To reach the trailhead from the small town of Crescent Lake, located on Oregon Highway 58, 35 miles southeast of Oakridge, travel southwest on paved Crescent Lake Road to a junction at 2.3 miles; turn right on paved Forest Road 60. The road passes by the north end of Crescent Lake, leading to the junction of Forest Road 6010, another 5.1 miles down the road.

Turn right onto Road 6010, traveling the unmaintained road (passenger cars okay) to Emigrant Pass, another 6.6 miles away. Summit Lake and campground are to your left as you head right on Forest Road 380; after 2.3 miles turn right on Forest Road 2160. Drive 4.1 miles until you reach Forest Road 2149 and a sign "Bear Mountain." Keep to the right on Road 2149, driving another 9.1

Diamond View Lake, Diamond Peak Wilderness.

Banana slug.

INTRODUCTION TO THE DRIFT CREEK WILDERNESS

The Drift Creek Wilderness is a land of plenty. There are steep-sided canyons, abundant wildlife, and a tremendous stand of old-growth rain forest. While horseback riding is prohibited due to the fragile soil, the preserve is a hiker's mecca.

At one time this was a mecca for the Alsea Indians as well. The Waldport-based Indians hunted here regularly and also gathered berries and other edibles. Later (prior to World War II), the white man appeared and tried, but did not successfully homestead the meadow you'll pass through while hiking the Drift Creek Wilderness.

Designated wilderness in 1984 with the signing of the Oregon Wilderness Act, few trails penetrate the 5,798-acre preserve. Ranging in elevation from a low of 120 feet along Drift Creek to 1,605 feet atop a nameless peak, the preserve lies 12 miles east of Waldport and 57 miles west of Corvallis.

Mild temperatures prevail year-round. Snow is rare, but rain is not. Heavy rainfall normally occurs from fall through spring, with 120 inches pelting Table Mountain. A mere 74 inches falls to the west.

Sitka spruce, Douglas-fir and western hemlock dominant the region. Growing seven feet thick in some places, many of the largest trees are found along the Horse Creek Trail. Bigleaf maple trees line the creeks. Moss, licorice ferns, sourgrass, oxalis and other plants blanket the forest floor. During the summer, look for scrumptious berries including salmonberry, thimbleberry, huckleberries (both the red and blue varieties), and salal. Roosevelt elk, black-tailed deer and black bear inhabit the forest surrounding Drift Creek. The northern spotted owl nests here

miles to the junction of Forest Road 23 and a sign: "Vivian Lake - 4 miles." Turn right on Road 23 and reach the trailhead near Hemlock Butte after 4.1 miles.

Trail info: A terrific view of Diamond Peak greets you as you begin hiking Vivian Lake Trail 3662, passing Notch Lake and a couple of other unnamed lakes as you ascend to the junction to Mount Yoran and Vivian Lake at 0.9 mile. Keep to the right on Mount Yoran Trail 3683, reaching a saddle at 2.5 miles. To the north you'll see the Three Sisters, Broken Top, and Mount Washington. And on a clear day it's possible to see the outline of Oregon's highest peak, Mount Hood. Reach Divide Lake at 4.0 miles.

VIVIAN LAKE (hike 13)

Trail length: About 3.8 miles one-way.
Description: A day hike in the Diamond Peak Wilderness.
Difficulty: Moderate.
Highlights: Wildflowers in June and July; fishing.
Elevations: 5,280 to 6,000 feet.
Maps: Diamond Peak Wilderness Map.
Hiking season: July through October.
Permits: Wilderness Permit; Trail Park Permit.
Contact: Rigdon Ranger Station, P.O. Box 1410, Oakridge, OR 97463; (541) 782-2283.
Directions: To reach the trailhead near Hemlock Butte, travel 35 miles southeast of Oakridge via Oregon Highway 58 to the small town of Crescent Lake. Head southwest on paved Crescent Lake Road and reach a junction of Forest Road 60 at 2.3 miles. Turn right at the sign: "Summit Lake - 12 miles." Drive the paved road along the north end of Crescent Lake to the junction of Forest Road 6010, another 5.1 miles down the road.

Turn right onto Road 6010, traveling the unmaintained dirt road (passenger cars okay) to Emigrant Pass, another 6.6 miles away. Summit Lake and campground are to your left as you head right on Forest Road 380. Soon after, pass the Pacific Crest Trailhead.

Continue for another mile or so then the road turns to a good gravel road. At 2.3 miles from Emigrant Pass turn right on Forest Road 2160. Drive 4.1 miles on this road until you reach Forest Road 2149 and a sign "Bear Mountain." Head to the right and continue traveling Road 2149. Notice the waterfall on the right, as you drive another 9.1 miles to the junction of Forest Road 23 and a sign: "Vivian Lake -4 miles." Turn right on Road 23 and reach the trail head near Hemlock Butte after 4.1 miles.

Trail info: A fantastic view of Diamond Peak welcomes you as you begin hiking Vivian Lake Trail 3662, ascending past Notch Lake to a junction at 0.9 mile. Head to the left, staying on the Vivian Lake Trail. You'll pass a couple of lakes as you continue to some wonderful cascades along Fall Creek, and the wildflower-blessed shore of Vivian Lake.

Drift Creek Wilderness.

River otter in a tree.

and our nation's symbol, the American bald eagle, has been sighted on occasion.

Huge runs of Chinook salmon, coho salmon, steelhead and cutthroat trout are found in Drift Creek, a tributary of the Alsea River. The fishing is excellent and is managed for native fish only. This region is also a moderately popular hunting area during the proper season.

HARRIS RANCH (hike 14)

Trail length: About 3.2 miles one-way.
Description: A day hike in the Drift Creek Wilderness.
Difficulty: Moderate.
Highlights: Fishing; old-growth forest; wildflower-blessed meadows.
Elevations: 1,250 to 160 feet.
Maps: Drift Creek Wilderness Map.
Hiking season: Year-round.
Permits: None required.
Contact: Waldport Ranger District, P.O. Box 400, Waldport, OR 97394; (541) 563-3211.
Directions: Reach the Harris Ranch Trailhead by driving 7.1 miles east of Waldport via County Road 34. Cross the Alsea River and turn left, now traveling north on Risley Creek Road (Forest Road 3446). Continue 4.1 miles to Forest Road 346; turn north and reach a fork in 0.7 mile and stay to the left, reaching the trailhead another 0.2 mile down the road.
Trail info: It's a short, gradual climb then a moderate, sometimes steep descent through lush old-growth forest of Douglas-fir, western hemlock, and cedar. The forest floor is carpeted with red huckleberry, vine maple, salmonberry, salal, foxglove, and trillium.

Reach Drift Creek Meadow at 2.2 miles. Before the meadow look to the right and see an old fireplace, now covered with moss, banana slugs, and daffodils. Not much more remains of the old Harris Ranch homestead. According to Forest Service records, Fred Purath, a bachelor, operated a subsistence type farm in this location. Purath, a loner, ran a few head of cattle, and walked into town but once a year. Earl Harris purchased the land in the early 1940s.

After entering the meadow you'll see two trails. The Harris Ranch Trail heads south 0.2 mile across the meadow, back into the

trees, and bumps into Drift Creek. Ford the creek and continue along the creek 0.8 mile farther to both the North and South Horse Creek Trails. (See HORSE CREEK TRAIL for more information.)

Those with two cars may want to park one at the South Horse Creek Trailhead, hike down the steeper Harris Ranch Trail, and hike back via the easier trail.) Please note, the Forest Service recommends crossing Drift Creek—which you'll do several times—during the summer months when the water level is low.

HORSE CREEK (hike 15)

Trail length: About 5.5 miles one-way.
Description: A day hike in the Drift Creek Wilderness.
Difficulty: Moderate.
Highlights: Old-growth forest; fishing.
Elevations: 1,600 to 200 feet.
Maps: Drift Creek Wilderness Map.
Hiking season: Year-round.
Permits: None required.
Contact: Waldport Ranger District, P.O. Box 400, Waldport, OR 97394; (541) 563-3211.
Directions: There are two Horse Creek Trailheads leading into the wilderness. You can decide whether to hike the whole trail via shuttle, or hike to Drift Creek and back via the north trailhead and then the south trailhead.

Reach the northern trailhead by traveling 0.8 mile north of Yachats; from U.S. Highway 101, head east on Bayview Road (County Road 701). After 5.2 miles reach North Bayview Road; stay to the left, driving another 1.0 mile to a fork. Head left on paved (and later gravel) Forest Road 51. Reach a fork after 5.8 miles; keep right, driving towards North Beaver Creek and Toledo. At 1.1 miles Road 51 curves to the left; stay straight, now driving paved Forest Road 50. Drive another 1.4 miles and turn right on gravel Forest Road 5087. Reach the trailhead in 3.5 miles.

To reach the southern trailhead use the directions listed for the Harris Ranch Trailhead. Continue east 4.5 miles to Forest Road 3464; turn left (north) and continue to the end of the road and trailhead at 1.6 miles.
Trail info: From the northern trailhead, descend gradually and then moderately to Drift Creek at 3.2 miles. Just prior to reaching the creek, you'll come to a fork. Head to the left for 50 yards for a good view of the creek and a nice place for a picnic. If you'd like to continue to the southern Horse Creek Trailhead, you'll have to ford the creek. The Forest Service claims Drift Creek can be forded during most summer months. Reach the southern trailhead after ascending 2.3 miles.

American coot on a nest.

INTRODUCTION TO THE EAGLE CAP WILDERNESS

The Eagle Cap Wilderness! A land of high granite peaks, alpine lakes and meadows, steep glaciated valleys, abundant wildlife, and delicate wildflowers.

Comprised of most of the Wallowa Mountain Range, a spur of the Blue Mountains of northeastern Oregon, the Eagle Cap Wilderness is surrounded by Hells Canyon National Recreation Area and other Wallowa-Whitman National Forest lands.

Managed exclusively by the Wallowa-Whitman National Forest, the wilderness was originally established as such on October 7, 1940. At that time, 220,000 acres were set aside. Later, Eagle Cap became part of the National Wilderness Preservation System under the Wilderness Act of 1964.

Today Oregon's largest wilderness consists of 358,461 acres with over 500 miles of trail providing access to this stunning area. Hikers can climb to the top of some of the highest peaks in the Wallowas, relax by 58 popular lakes or one of the many unnamed small lakes or tarns, and those who enjoy bushwhacking can hike to their heart's content.

Anglers will find good fishing in many area lakes with eastern brook, rainbow, or golden trout available. Also, there are four major rivers—the Minam, Lostine, Wallowa, and Imnaha—to fish, as well as numerous creeks and streams. Rock climbers will find several opportunities for climbing with Eagle Cap Peak, Matterhorn, and Sacajawea being the most popular. Those in search of a less crowded peak to climb should note that there are 31 peaks over 8,000 feet in elevation. Two peaks, Matterhorn and Sacajawea, soar to nearly 10,000 feet, 15 more climb to over 9,000 feet, and 14 others reach more than 8,000 feet.

While hiking the many trails throughout the area, note that many trails originated from wildlife and American Indian paths. Used as hunting and plant gathering grounds, Native Americans did not live in the area year-round because of the harsh conditions. In the late 1800's, the trails were improved by sheepmen, trappers, and prospectors. Today, mining relics can be found in some areas.

While hiking has proven to be the most popular wilderness pastime, there are other activities to enjoy. Besides fishing and rock climbing, there are horseback riding, photography, and during the winter months, cross-country skiing and snowshoeing. Wildlife viewing and plant study add to a true wilderness experience.

Supporting nearly every plant community present in the Blue Mountains, the wilderness is truly a plant-lover's delight. At lower elevations see bunchgrass and sagebrush. Higher up look for spruce, subalpine fir, and grouse huckleberry; also, there are ponderosa pine, mountain hemlock, and several small stands of limber pine. Above treeline plant communities are dominated by subalpine shrubs, heather, sedges, and fragile alpine plants.

Ranging from a low of 4,000 to 5,000 feet along the lower river drainages to a high of 9,839 feet atop Sacajawea Mountain, the wilderness embraces a variety of habitat types, suitable for native wildlife. Elk or deer may be seen in most parts of the area. Other species include black bear, cougar, bobcat, bighorn sheep, coyotes, bats, hoary marmots, flying squirrels, porcupine, otter, beaver, badgers, and wolverine. Also, there are mountain goats. Introduced on Chief Joseph Mountain in March of 1950, the goats are most often seen at Chief Joseph Mountain, Ice Lake, the Matterhorn, and Sacajawea Peak.

Bird life is impressive with blue grouse, Clark's nutcrackers, and a variety of species of woodpeckers, owls, and sandpipers sighted. Peregrine falcons have also been observed. Other raptors include both bald and golden eagles, Swainson's hawks, and ferruginous hawks.

Eagle Cap Wilderness is usually accessible by the Fourth of July, but mountain passes often support snowdrifts until August. The hiking season is short, with heavy snows by late October. Temperatures vary in the summer with highs warming to the 90's and dropping to the 40's at night. Visitors should be prepared for sudden changes in the weather and look out for late-afternoon thunderstorms.

EAGLE LAKE (hike 16)

Trail length: About 7.4 miles one-way.
Description: A long day hike or a backpack trip into the Eagle Cap Wild.
Difficulty: Moderate.
Highlights: Meadows; abundant wildflowers; fishing.
Elevations: 4,991 to 7,520 feet.
Maps: Eagle Cap Wilderness Map.
Hiking season: July through October.
Permits: Wilderness permit; limit group size to 12.
Contact: Wallowa Mountains Visitor Center, 88401 Hwy. 82, Enterprise, OR 97828; (541) 426-5546.
Directions: Reach the Main Eagle Creek Trailhead by driving from Medical Springs; turn right in town, heading south on Collins Road. After 1.6 miles go left on Forest Road 67; drive 13 miles to the junction of Forest Road 77. Make another left and continue up Forest Road 77 to a fork at 0.7 mile. Turn right, driving Forest Road 7755 for 3.7 miles to the trailhead.
Trail info: From the trailhead hike Main Eagle Creek Trail 1922, crossing Eagle Creek at 0.3 mile. There are several more creek crossings as you continue up to Copper Creek at 2.5 miles. (Notice Copper Creek Falls just ahead and to the left.)

Reach a junction at 2.8 miles; the trail to the left heads to Bench Canyon, the one on the right leads to Eagle Lake. You'll come to another junction at 4.3 miles; the trail to the right leads to Lookingglass Lake which is described in this guide. Keep to the left, crossing more creeks and enjoying a view of Needlepoint Mountain (9,032 feet) at various points along the way. Reach yet another junction at 6.2 miles; make a right and meet Eagle Lake at 7.4 miles.

ECHO LAKE/TRAVERSE LAKE (hike 17)

Trail length: About 7.3 miles one-way.
Description: A long day hike or a backpack trip into the Eagle Cap Wilderness.
Difficulty: Moderate.
Highlights: Magnificent views; abundant wildflowers; good swimming; fishing.
Elevations: 5,570 to 7,760 feet.
Maps: Eagle Cap Wilderness Map.
Hiking season: July through October.
Permits: Wilderness permit; limit group size to 12.
Contact: Wallowa Mountains Visitor Center, 88401 Hwy. 82, Enterprise, OR 97828; (541) 426-5546.
Directions: Reach the West Eagle Creek Trailhead by driving Oregon Highway 203 south from the small town of Union. Turn left onto Forest Road 77 at 13.0 miles. (A well-maintained gravel road for the first 10.0 miles, Road 77 turns into a rough dirt road after that. A sign recommends that passenger cars not attempt the trip.) Reach West Eagle Meadow, 14.3 miles from Oregon 203; turn left, reaching the trailhead in 0.3 mile.

*Facing page: Backpacker and her samoyed at Swamp Lake, Eagle Cap Wilderness. **Below:** Bighorn sheep (rams).*

Trail info: Begin an easy hike through the trees along West Eagle Creek Trail 1934, passing the junction to Trail 1914 en route. Cross the frigid waters of Fake Creek at 0.4 mile and several other small streams before crossing West Eagle Creek at 0.8 mile. Now the trail appears to continue up the creek, but it doesn't. Instead, after fording the creek you'll cross a meadow, eventually hiking across an open slope where there are many kinds of wildflowers.

At 2.2 miles come to a creek (it's your last chance for water for nearly three miles). Cross it then switchback up to Trail 1943 junction, which heads left to Elk Creek, at 2.8 miles; keep to the right.

Reach the fast-flowing waters of West Eagle Creek at 4.9 miles. Cross the creek, following the trail to a small unnamed lake at 5.1 miles. Continue on to Echo Lake at 5.6 miles. Pass a spring at 6.9 miles, now hiking across a granite slope to Traverse Lake at 7.3 miles.

JIM WHITE RIDGE LOOP (hike 18)

Trail length: About 21.4 miles for the complete loop.
Description: An extended backpack trip into the Eagle Cap Wilderness.
Difficulty: Moderate to strenuous.
Highlights: Solitude; nice views; wildlife.
Elevations: 4,800 to 7,440 feet.
Maps: Eagle Cap Wilderness Map.
Hiking season: July through October.
Permits: Wilderness Permit; limit group size to 12.
Contact: Wallowa Mountains Visitor Center, 88401 Hwy. 82, Enterprise, OR 97828; (541) 426-5546.
Directions: To reach the Moss Spring Trailhead, drive to Cove, located 16 miles east of La Grande. Turn east off Oregon Highway 237 at the sign for "Moss Springs Campground." The road you're traveling is Forest Road 6220. Continue on to a fork 0.3 mile down the road; head right, driving 5.0 miles to a fork and the entrance to the campground. Make a right, driving through the campground to the trail head 0.2 mile away.
Trail info: Begin hiking at the Moss Spring Trailhead sign, heading east to a fork 100 yards down the trail; Little Minam River is to the right, Minam River to the left. Head to the right (counter-clockwise) for the easiest loop which will end by hiking the trail to the left.

Hike through the trees, reaching Fireline Creek at 1.2 miles. Continue to the unsigned junction of Trail 1913 at 2.0 miles. Cross a creek, the Little Minam River, and many streams as you proceed to a junction at 7.8 miles. Rock Creek Trail heads to the east; hike north to Jim White Ridge.

Come to the unsigned junction of Pot Creek at 8.2 miles and the signed junction to Little Pot Creek Trail 1919 at 8.9 miles. Shortly thereafter come to a fork. Head to the right, following rock cairns up a ridge and across a saddle to Jim White Ridge. Follow blazed trees when the trail isn't obvious.

Reach the junction of the Minam River Trail and Moss Spring Trail 1908 at 17.0 miles. Head straight 100 yards and across the bridge over Little Minan River, continuing back to the trailhead at 21.4 miles.

LOOKINGGLASS LAKE (hike 19)

Trail length: About 7.4 miles one-way.
Description: A long day hike or an overnight backpack trip into the Eagle Cap Wilderness.
Difficulty: Moderate to strenuous.
Highlights: Grand views; wildflowers; fishing.
Elevations: 5,231 to 7,360 feet.
Maps: Eagle Cap Wilderness Map.
Hiking season: July through October.
Permits: Wilderness Permit; limit group size to 12.
Contact: Wallowa Mountains Visitor Center, 88401 Hwy. 82, Enterprise, OR 97828; (541) 426-5546.
Directions: Reach the Main Eagle Creek Trailhead by driving to Medical Springs. From here, head south on Collins Road for 1.6 miles then go left on Forest Road 67; drive 13.0 miles to the junction of Forest Road 77. Make a left on Road 77, reaching a fork after 0.7 mile; turn right, now driving Forest Road 7755 for 3.7 miles to the trailhead.

Porcupine.

Trail info: From the trailhead, hike Main Eagle Creek Trail 1922, crossing Eagle Creek at 0.3 mile. Cross several streams and hike through an open meadow before fording Copper Creek at 2.5 miles. Be sure to look for Copper Creek Falls, a short ways down the trail and to the left.

Reach a junction at 2.8 miles; the trail on the left leads to Bench Canyon. Stay to the right to reach Lookingglass Lake. You'll come to another junction at 4.3 miles. The trail to the left leads to Eagle Lake, which is described in this guide. Keep right to reach Lookingglass Lake, crossing several streams as you continue to the lake at 7.4 miles.

PINE LAKES (hike 20)

Trail length: About 7.5 miles one-way.
Description: A long day hike or a backpack trip into the Eagle Cap Wilderness.
Difficulty: Moderate.
Highlights: Splendid views; animal life including pikas; and two scenic lakes.
Elevations: 4,830 to 7,520 feet.
Maps: Eagle Cap Wilderness Map.
Hiking season: July through October.
Permits: Wilderness permit; limit group size to 12.
Contact: Wallowa Mountains Visitor Center, 88401 Hwy. 82, Enterprise, OR 97828; (541) 426-5546.
Directions: To reach the trailhead at Cornucopia drive north on Main Street in downtown Halfway. The road is paved for the first 5.3 miles then turns to gravel and is quite bumpy. A sign warns "Road steep, windy, slippery when wet," but is usually passable with a passenger car. Reach a fork 10.3 miles from Halfway. Head right to the Cornucopia Pack Station 0.5 mile away. At the pack station the road forks; go left and park near the Pine Lakes sign.
Trail info: Hike Pine Lakes Trail 1880 (a dirt road), then ford East Fork Creek at 0.2 mile. Ford another stream shortly thereafter, then hike along the east side of West Pine Creek. Cross West Pine Creek via bridges at both 0.9 mile and 1.9 miles.

You'll climb moderately across, spending most of your time on open slopes before reaching another stream at 4.8 miles. As you continue, look for a waterfall on the north ridge; Pine Lakes is located above the falls.

At 5.5 miles the trail passes through the trees and across a stream which is flowing from the falls. Reach the smaller of the two Pine Lakes at 7.5 miles. The larger of the two Pine Lakes is located just to the west of the smaller lake.

The lakes are excellent for swimming and fishing, ranging in depth from 35 to 70 feet deep. Both are stocked with eastern brook trout.

SWAMP LAKE LOOP (hike 21)

Trail length: About 31.5 miles for the complete loop.
Description: An extended backpack trip into the Eagle Cap Wilderness.
Difficulty: Moderate to strenuous.
Highlights: Spectacular views; lovely alpine lakes; the chance for solitude.
Elevations: 5,060 to 8,560 feet.
Maps: Eagle Cap Wilderness Map.
Hiking season: July through October.
Permits: Wilderness Permit; limit group size to 12.
Contact: Wallowa Mountains Visitor Center, 88401 Hwy. 82, Enterprise, OR 97828; (541) 426-5546.
Directions: To reach the trailhead drive Oregon Highway 82 to Lostine. Head south at the sign "Lostine River Campgrounds." The paved road turns to gravel at 7.0 miles and becomes Forest Road 8210, a rough, bumpy road, leading to the Bowman Trailhead, another 8.0 miles up the road. Begin the loop here or at the East Fork Lostine Trailhead (where I began this loop) 3.8 miles farther.
Trail info: Begin hiking at the trailhead which leads to both East Fork Lostine Trail 1662 and Minam Lake Trail 1670. After 0.1 mile stay right on Minam Lake Trail 1670.

Reach a junction at 2.8 miles and go right via Trail 1656. You'll come to a junction at 7.8 miles; take the right fork, Trail 1675, towards the North Minam River.

At 9.7 miles reach the north end of Swamp Lake and the junction to Long Lake, via Trail 1669. Keep on the trail to the right and head up the slope to the top of the ridge and a wonderful view of Steamboat Lake at 10.1 miles.

Reach the North Minam River at 16.9 miles and follow the trail as it winds along North Minam Meadow to your left; Continue to Wilson Basin at 17.4 miles. Turn right, hiking Bowman Trail 1651. At 21.2 miles reach the unsigned junction to John Henry Lake. It's a mere 0.4 mile away.

To complete the loop, continue on, reaching a junction at 24.1 miles. Chimney Lake is to your left, Lostine Canyon straight ahead. Stay straight, crossing Bowman Creek several times en route to the bridge over the Lostine River. Reach the Bowman Creek Trailhead at 27.7 miles. Now it's an easy hike up the road 3.8 miles to the trail head at East Fork Lostine.

INTRODUCTION TO THE GEARHART MOUNTAIN WILDERNESS

Vertical walls of rock, delicate meadows, tall pines, wildlife and wildflowers, a sapphire blue lake, and breathtaking views make the Gearhart Mountain Wilderness a real treat.

Baby pronghorn.

Head of Dairy Creek, Gearhart Mountain Wilderness.

Located in the Fremont National Forest of south-central Oregon, the Gearhart Mountain Wilderness is 12 airline miles from Bly. Bly is the nearest town to the wilderness, providing supplies such as, gasoline, food, and other essentials.

The wilderness was first established by the Forest Service on November 11, 1943. Named the Gearhart Wild Area, and totaling 18,709 acres, the area was noted for its high elevation, scenic overlooks, and rock formations. It was also one of the few remaining roadless areas in this part of Oregon. In 1964, Congress passed the Wilderness Act, thus the Gearhart Wild Area was renamed the Gearhart Mountain Wilderness. Today, the wilderness consists of 22,809 acres, the extra acreage added by the Oregon Wilderness Act of 1984.

Gearhart Mountain, rising 8,354 feet above sea level, is certainly the most prominent feature in the wilderness. Formed by volcanic flows and plugs of porphyritic lava, scientists believe that this mountain was once a massive dome standing at least 10,000 feet high. As the land and climate cooled, ice formed. Enormous snowfields and glaciers blanketed the dome for thousands of years. Once again the land warmed, melting the ice, and carving the U-shaped valleys seen today.

There are three trails leading into the wilderness, all with special features of their own. But regardless of where you begin, all trails lead to Gearhart Mountain. As you approach the mountain notice that it appears to be split in two, both halves standing side-by-side. The northern most half is called "The Notch" and breaks off from the main peak for more than 300 feet.

When viewing Gearhart Mountain from the east the sheer rock cliffs make a summit climb without the use of technical mountaineering equipment seem all but impossible. Although there isn't a trail leading to the top, the summit can be reached by climbing the dominant south ridge. From Gearhart's highest point you'll see, on a clear day, Steens Mountain to the east, Blue Lake to the northeast, and towards the west you'll gaze at a variety of Cascade Peaks extending from Mt. Lassen in California to the Three Sisters in Oregon.

Observing plant life and animals are always an added plus when hiking in the wilderness and the Gearhart Mountain Wilderness is no exception. During spring and early summer wildflowers splash their bright colors

American bumble bee.

lake in the wilderness. To continue on to the marsh, hike around the southwest end of the lake and then proceed along the fairly level trail to the marsh at 3.9 miles. Be sure to look for Rocky Mountain elk, especially during the summer and fall months, when a herd of about 30 to 50 animals wander in and out of the area.

Those of you who'd like to continue up the trail may do so. It's another 3.5 miles or so to the high point along the Gearhart Trail and access to the Notch. See GEARHART TRAIL, for more information.

GEARHART TRAIL (hike 23)

Trail length: About 6.0 miles one-way.
Description: A long day hike or an overnight backpack into the Gearhart Mountain Wilderness.
Difficulty: Moderate to strenuous.
Highlights: Unique rock formations; see-forever views; wildlife; wild flowers.
Elevations: 6,508 to 8,040 feet.
Maps: Gearhart Mountain Wilderness Map.
Hiking season: Mid-June through early November.
Permits: None required, but please register at trailhead; limit group size to 12 people.
Contact: Bly Ranger District, Bly, OR 97622; (541) 353-2427.
Directions: From Bly, drive one mile east on Oregon Highway 140. Turn left (north) on Campbell Road. After about 0.5 mile, make a right on Forest Road 34. Continue 14.4 miles to Forest Road 012; follow the one-way dirt road 1.4 miles to the Lookout Rock Trailhead.
Trail info: Although there are several trails leading to a point near The Notch (The Notch denotes the top of Gearhart Mountain which is split in two, the Notch being estranged from the main peak for more than 300 feet), the following route is the most scenic.

Soon after entering the wilderness you'll pass the Palisades, strange rock formations born of massive porphyritic lava flows. Ponderosa pines stand scattered throughout the rocky terrain as you continue past the Dome, an striking group of cliffs rising up to 400 feet above the surrounding terrain.

As you continue, look for California's Mount Shasta, more than 100 miles away. The trail descends from the saddle to Dairy Creek, passing through a wildflower-blessed meadow with 8,364-foot Gearhart Mountain in the background.

You'll reach the highest point of the trail at about 6 miles. From here you can scramble another 300 feet to the top; see Steens Mountain to the east, a variety of Cascade Peaks from California's Mount Lassen to Oregon's Three Sisters to the west, and Blue Lake to the northeast.

Please note, Gearhart Trail continues north for another 7.5 miles to the North Fork Trailhead. See the BLUE LAKE/GEARHART MARSH TRAIL for more information.

against the lush green meadows, like a child with her first set of finger paints. And if you're one of the lucky ones you may catch a glimpse of a trophy buck walking silently through the woods, or hear a bull elk bugling during the crisp days of autumn. Maybe you'll see a mountain lion, a bear, a bobcat or a coyote. Birdwatchers might see a variety of warblers, woodpeckers, jays, or owls and perhaps a blue grouse, or two or three.

You may see cattle grazing in parts of the wilderness. Unfortunately, the loss of vegetation due to heavy browsing on riparian shrubs is evident in some areas. Don't add to the destruction. Remember, "leave only footprints, take only memories."

BLUE LAKE/GEARHART MARSH (hike 22)

Trail length: About 3.9 miles one-way.
Description: A day hike or an overnight backpack into the Gearhart Mountain Wilderness.
Difficulty: Easy to moderate.
Highlights: Fishing at Blue lake; watching Rocky Mountain elk and other animal life in Gearhart Marsh.
Elevations: 6,340 to 6,900 feet.
Maps: Gearhart Mountain Wilderness Map.
Hiking season: Mid-June through early November.
Permits: None required, but please register at trailhead; limit group size to 12 people.
Contact: Bly Ranger District, Bly, OR 97622; (541) 353-2427.
Directions: From Bly, drive one mile east on Oregon Highway 140; make a left on Campbell Road. Drive about 0.5 mile to Forest Road 34; make a right and continue for 19.3 miles to Road 3372. Now go left for about 9 miles to Road 015; turn left and follow the road about 1.5 miles to the North Fork Trailhead.
Trail info: The trail winds through open pine and thick stands of fir and lodgepole pine, with small meadows an occasional delight. It's an easy 3-mile hike to Blue Lake, a popular fishing spot, and the only

Common raven.

INTRODUCTION TO THE GRASSY KNOB WILDERNESS

The Grassy Knob Wilderness is located in the Coast Range, a few miles east of Port Orford and less than ten miles from the Pacific Ocean. Established as wilderness with the passage of the Oregon Wilderness Act of 1984, Grassy Knob came to be for several reasons, but primarily to protect the immensely valuable anadromous fishery.

Extremely steep and rugged, the wilderness consists of 17,200 acres managed by the Siskiyou National Forest. In addition to being extremely steep and rugged, the area is also thickly forested. Several rocky bluffs provide but a few openings from which the wilderness can be observed. As a result, few humans will ever see much of the area, rich in some very large and majestic old-growth forests of Port Orford cedar, Douglas-fir, hemlock, and western redcedar.

Elevation in the Grassy Knob Wilderness ranges from a low of 100 feet on the Elk River, located in the southern portion of the preserve to a high of 2,474 feet atop Anvil Mountain, located near the heart of the wilderness.

Wilderness creeks and streams drain into two highly scenic coastal streams, the Elk River and Dry Creek. Steep-sided gorges, clear water, along with good salmon and steelhead fishing make the streams quite popular, especially in the fall and spring, when anadromous fish return to spawn in the river and its tributaries.

Nesting pairs of spotted owls have been found in the area. This wilderness provides ideal old-growth habitat for these medium-sized, dark-eyed owls, whose doglike barks and cries penetrate deep into the forest.

Before Grassy Knob was designated wilderness two roads were built into the area. Now the roads are closed at the wilderness boundary and serve as trails. The only true trail in the wilderness, a 150 yard trail leading to the site of the old Grassy Knob Lookout, is located near Grassy Knob. See GRASSY KNOB for more information.

Today the lookout is gone, but the view is quite nice. From this point it's possible to see the surrounding pine-covered mountains, as well as, waves breaking on the beautiful Pacific Coastline.

The lookout was removed in the 1960s because other lookouts were able to cover the area much better. A bit of interesting history surrounds the lookout at Grassy Knob. During World War II, a plane, launched from a Japanese submarine, flew inland. It was seen by two lookouts, one of which was Grassy Knob. Some even say the Japanese aircraft was shot at from the lookout. Oregon author, Bert Webber, gives a full account of the unusual event in his book entitled, *Retaliation*.

The steep and rugged terrain associated with the Grassy Knob Wilderness may be difficult to hike in, but it can be viewed easily from the top of Grassy Knob. And because the area gets little use each hiker should be able to enjoy the view all by themselves.

Moss on tree.

Pacific tree frog.

GRASSY KNOB (hike 24)

Trail length: About 0.5 mile one-way.
Description: A short day hike in the Grassy Knob Wilderness.
Difficulty: Easy.
Highlights: Solitude; view of the Pacific Ocean; old-growth forest, historic area.
Elevations: 2,192 to 2,342.
Maps: Port Orford 15-minute USGS quad.
Hiking season: All year.
Permits: None required.
Contact: Powers Ranger District, Powers, OR 97466;(541) 439-3011.
Directions: Drive 3 miles north of Port Orford on U.S. Highway 101 then head east on Grassy Knob Road (Curry County Road 196). The road is paved for the first four miles then turns to a well-maintained gravel road. When pavement turns to gravel, take Forest Road 5105 until it ends at 8.0 miles.
Trail info: The trail is located at the east end of the parking area. A sign is posted to point you in the right direction. Cross the barricade and follow the road until it begins to level off, about 0.5 mile. Just before you reach the crest, walk up the bank to the right. The trail is unmarked. The trail leads to the southwest for 50 feet or so then to the southeast for another 50 feet. Once you reach this point the trail is easy to find. Follow it 150 yards to the top of Grassy Knob. From this point there is a wonderful 180-degree view.

INTRODUCTION TO THE HELLS CANYON WILDERNESS

Hells Canyon! It's the deepest gorge in North America, and according to the Guinness Book of World Records, it's "the deepest canyon in low relief territory." From atop Seven Devils Mountain in Idaho, Hells Canyon plunges an amazing 7,900 feet to the mighty Snake River. In between the high mountains and low-lying river there's a world of steep cliffs, and bunchgrass plateaus. It's a place where elk, deer, bear, mountain goats, mountain lion, and bighorn sheep roam. A place where eagles soar on high, and falcons dive on unsuspecting prey.

Set apart from most of the other areas listed in this guide, Hells Canyon Wilderness is unusual in that it's part of a larger protected area, the Hells Canyon National Recreation Area (NRA). Established by Congress in 1975, Hells Canyon NRA straddles the Hells Canyon of the Snake River, stretching west to the mountain slopes of northeast Oregon, and east to the peaks of west central Idaho's Seven Devils Mountains.

Hells Canyon NRA consists of a total of 652,488 acres, 216,832 acres of which have been designated wilderness. Much of the current wilderness was designated as such when Congress established the NRA in 1975. Additional acreage, however, was added with the passage of the Oregon Wilderness Act of 1984.

As mentioned previously, the wilderness blankets a portion of two states, 130,095 acres of which are located in Oregon. (Because this book deals with Oregon's wilderness areas, Idaho's trails were not traveled.)

The Wallowa-Whitman National Forest manages both the NRA and wilderness, and maintains nearly 1,000 miles of trail which penetrate the area, 352 miles of which lead into the wilderness.

Three National Recreation Trails and one National Historic Trail traverse the NRA. The Nee-Me-Poo Trail, a National Historic Trail, is found on the Oregon side and is included in this guidebook.

Trails lead across side canyons, over grassy benchlands, through timbered ridgetops, and down to the Snake River. Although the Snake River is not included as part of the Hells Canyon Wilderness, it is designated as a Wild and Scenic River. The Wild and Scenic portion of the river extends 31.5 river miles. The 17 miles from Hells Canyon Dam to Johnson Bar are exceptionally steep. Here, the river is at its best, boasting some of the largest white water rapids in all of North America.

At the opposite end of the scale is 6,982-foot Hat Point, a popular place where visitors can gaze down at the Snake River, winding along more than a mile below.

Visitors will find portions of Hells Canyon accessible year-round. The Forest Service, though, recommends spring, late summer and early fall, as the best times for backpacking. Those that crave few crowds and uncrowded camp areas, however, should avoid hiking into Hells Canyon in October for hunting season is in full force.

Daytime temperatures during the summer average 90 degrees and water can be quite scarce so enter the area fully prepared. Spring and fall are cooler. Hikers should be alert for rattlesnakes and black widow spiders. Poison oak is something else you should avoid. Look for this shiny, three-leaved plant along the lower reaches of Hells Canyon.

Plant species are as varied as the terrain. At the lowest altitudes, shrubs and grasses are predominant with an occasional ponderosa pine found on exposed streamsides. White alder, box elder, and water birch are common along streamsides. Farther up the slopes there are a variety of bunchgrass species. Above 4,000 feet you'll find dense stands of Douglas-fir, along with ponderosa and ninebark pine. Grand fir and sub-alpine fir associations are generally found above 5,000 feet.

When some folks think of Hells Canyon and the Snake River, they think of rafting down busy rapids. While rafting is certainly a favorite, others opt to see the river via jet boat, while others day hike, and still others decide to backpack. There are also those who come to fish, photograph, or ride horseback, and while they come for various reasons, they all have one thing in common. They came to experience the Hells Canyon Wilderness.

BEAR MOUNTAIN (hike 25)

Trail length: About 8.4 miles one-way.
Description: A long day hike or a backpack adventure in the Hells Canyon Wilderness.
Difficulty: Moderate to strenuous.
Highlights: See-forever views.

Horsemen at Hells Canyon Wilderness.

Elevations: 3,600 to 6,895 feet.
Maps: Hells Canyon National Recreation Area Map.
Hiking season: June through October.
Permits: Trail Park Permit.
Contact: Wallowa Mountains Visitor Center, 88401 Hwy. 82, Enterprise, OR 97828; (541) 426-5546.
Directions: To reach the Freezeout Trailhead, drive from the intersection of Oregon Highway 82 and Wallowa Road in Joseph. Go east on Wallowa Road for 30 miles to Imnaha. Turn right on Upper Imnaha Road (County Road 727), a gravel road which leads south to Forest Road 4230 in 12.7 miles; turn left on Road 4230, driving this good dirt road to the trailhead at 3.0 miles.
Trail info: Hike Saddle Creek Trail 1776 to the junction of Western Rim Trail 1774 at 2.2 miles; make a right, heading south on the Western Rim Trail. There's a grand view from here: To the east you'll see the summits of both Bear Mountain and Black Mountain; Saddle Creek drainage is to the northeast; Hat Point is to the north.

You'll meet up with another trail at 3.3 miles. Keep to the trail on the left. Reach the junction to Trail 1763 at 5.0 miles; stay on Trail 1774, arriving at the Bear Mountain Trail junction at 5.9 miles.

To continue to Bear Mountain, hike Bear Mountain Trail 1743 and reach the summit at 8.4 miles. From here the view is terrific. You'll see the Snake River drainage, the Seven Devils Mountains of Idaho, and Hat Point.

Those that desire may want to climb the summit of nearby Black Mountain. At 6,862 feet, the summit lies 0.8 mile away and can be reached by descending 495 feet then climbing 462 feet.

HAT POINT LOOP (hike 26)

Trail length: About 32.0 miles for the complete loop.
Description: A several day backpack adventure in the Hells Canyon Wilderness.
Difficulty: Moderate to very strenuous.
Highlights: Grand vistas; abundant wildlife; wildflowers. Watch for poison oak and rattlesnakes.
Elevations: 1,345 to 6,982 feet.
Maps: Hells Canyon National Recreation Area Map.
Hiking season: May through November; lower portions of the trail are snowfree most of the year.
Permits: Trail Park Permit.
Contact: Wallowa Mountains Visitor Center, 88401 Hwy. 82, Enterprise, OR 97828; (541) 426-5546.
Directions: To reach the Freezeout Trailhead from the junction of Oregon Highway 82 and Wallowa Road in Joseph, travel east on Wallowa Road for 30 miles to Imnaha. Turn right on Upper Imnaha Road (County Road 727), a gravel road which leads south to Forest Road 4230 in 12.7 miles; turn left on Road 4230, driving 3.0 miles to the trailhead.

Peregrine falcon.

Bighorn sheep (Ram).

Trail info: Hike Saddle Creek Trail 1776 to the junction of Western Rim Trail 1774 at 2.2 miles; continue straight down the drainage, reaching the Snake River at 9.5 miles.

Travel north along Snake River Trail 1726. Reach Sluice Creek at 14.5 miles. Head up Sluice Creek Trail 1748 to High Trail 1751 at 18.3 miles; going another 0.2 mile to Hat Creek and the junction to Hat Point.

Standing atop Hat Point, at 6,982 feet, is a must-do. Hike Hat Creek Trail 1752 to Hat Point, an additional 3.7 miles and 2,300 feet up. From Hat Point, you'll look down more than a mile into Hells Canyon.

If you'd rather not descend back to the High Trail (which is really very lovely), you can take a shortcut by walking Forest Roads 332, 315, and 4240. These roads also serve as the Western Rim National Recreation Trail 1774. Just past the Saddle Creek Campground, head left on Trail 1774, hiking to Freezeout Saddle, and back to the trailhead in 9.6 miles.

Back at the High Trail junction, continue on High Trail 1751. Reach the junction of Saddle Creek Trail at 26 miles. Go west on Saddle Creek Trail 1776, which leads to the trailhead.

MCGRAW CABIN LOOP (hike 27)

Trail length: About 14.2 miles for the complete loop.
Description: A long day hike or an overnight backpack trip in the Hells Canyon Wilderness.
Difficulty: Moderate to strenuous.
Highlights: Wildlife; wildflowers; close-up view of an old homestead, Hells Canyon, and the Snake River. Watch for poison oak and rattlesnakes.

Hells Canyon Wilderness.

Elevations: 1,769 to 3,360 feet.

Maps: Hells Canyon National Recreation Area Map.

Hiking season: Usually open all year, but occasionally closed due to snow.

Permits: None required.

Contact: Wallowa Mountains Visitor Center, 88401 Hwy. 82, Enterprise, OR 97828; (541) 426-5546.

Directions: There are two ways to reach the Hells Canyon Trailhead. From Baker, drive Oregon Highway 86 east for 70.0 miles. Upon reaching the Snake River, turn left on County Road 1039 and head past the sign leading to "Hells Canyon Trail." Reach the end of the road in 9.0 miles.

To reach the trailhead from Joseph, drive Wallowa Road from town (towards Imnaha), to the junction of Cloverdale Road at 8.3 miles. After 5.0 miles the road becomes Forest Road 39. Drive this to the junction of Oregon Highway 86, another 49.0 miles away. Turn left on Highway 86, reaching County Road 1039 in 7.2 miles. Proceed as mentioned above.

Trail info: Wildflowers are abundant in spring; watch for poison oak in the lower reaches of Spring and McGraw Creeks and along the Snake River all year.

Hike north via Hells Canyon Trail 1890, reaching McGraw Creek and a bridge at 2.1 miles. Continue on the Bench Trail 1884 or hike the loop in reverse by climbing up McGraw Creek Trail 1879 and descending Bench Trail. This loop heads up Bench Trail and down McGraw Creek Trail.

At 2.9 miles reach the junction to Bench Trail and head up it. If the trail is tough to find, look for the occasional rock cairn. Reach a junction and sign at 5.6 miles.

McGraw Cabin Trail is located just before the sign. Hike it past a nice stand of ponderosa pine trees at 7.4 miles. From the ponderosas, follow the trail to the McGraw Cabin at 9.3 miles.

After exploring the cabin, head to the left of the fence and to the left of the trail to McGraw Creek, which you'll cross on several occasions as you descend to Hells Canyon Trail at 12.1 miles; head right and back to the trailhead.

NEE-ME-POO TRAIL (hike 28)

Trail length: About 4.3 miles one-way.

Description: A day hike in the Hells Canyon Wilderness.

Difficulty: Moderate.

Highlights: Historic trail; cactus; nice views. Watch for poison oak and rattlesnakes.

Elevations: 2,640 to 1,000 feet.

Maps: Hells Canyon National Recreation Area Map.

Hiking season: Usually open 10 months, but occasionally closed due to snow.

Permits: None required.

Contact: Wallowa Mountains Visitor Center, 88401 Hwy. 82, Enterprise, OR 97828; (541) 426-5546.

Directions: Drive Wallowa Road east from Joseph, reaching Imnaha in 30 miles. Turn left (north) on paved Lower Imnaha Road and follow this to Forest Road 4260 at 6.5 miles. Continue 16.3 miles to the trailhead. (The road can be rocky, narrow, and steep. It is also slippery when wet; use four-wheel drive under these conditions.) If you have someone to pick you up at the opposite end of the trail continue another 7.8 miles to Dug Bar.

Trail info: From the west end of the trail, a sign points the way to Lone Pine Saddle at 1.2 miles. Reach Big Canyon Creek at 2.2 miles. Reach the east end of the trail, and the trailhead at Dug Bar, at 4.3 miles.

This is the historic site of the Nez Perce crossing in 1877. The Wallowa Valley was home to the Nez Perce and their ancestors for countless generations, but in the spring of 1877, General Howard of the U.S. Army ordered the Indians onto a reservation.

Reluctantly, Chief Joseph and his band of 400, including 64 braves, headed east to the Snake River, taking over 1,000 head of horses and cattle, but leaving much of their stock behind. The Nee-Me-Poo National Recreation Trail was but a small portion of the route they followed to the Snake.

After crossing the Snake River, Chief Joseph's band joined other bands of Nez Perce and a small group of Palouses. Soon after, the historical Nez Perce War began as the Indians fled to Canada where they hoped to find freedom. Their journey covered about 1,800 miles as they headed north, confusing and outwitting 2,000 troops of the U.S. Army. Burdened with small children, women, and the elderly throughout their journey, the Nez Perce were always able to outdistance the troops until they reached the Bear Paw Mountains of Montana, just 30 miles from the Canadian border. It was there, so close to freedom, that the Nez Perce were forced to surrender.

INTRODUCTION TO THE KALMIOPSIS WILDERNESS

Hikers who crave variety will no doubt find the Kalmiopsis Wilderness a most intriguing place. There is the Kalmiopsis leachiana, a rare plant for which the wilderness is named, there's the chance for a memorable hike to the top of Bald Mountain, the opportunity for a short hike across rocky, serpentine soil to Vulcan Lake, and more.

The Kalmiopsis Wilderness is located in southwest Oregon, approximately 30 miles east of the coastal town of Brookings. Straddling the Siskiyou Mountains of the Klamath Mountain Range, just north of the Oregon-California border, the wilderness reaches from a low elevation of 500 feet near the Illinois River to 5,098 feet atop Pearsoll Peak.

The Siskiyou National Forest manages the 179,700 acre preserve. One of the least known and least visited wilderness areas, the Kalmiopsis Wilderness was originally designated a primitive area in 1946. Eighteen years later, on September 3, 1964, the area became a unit of the National Wilderness Preservation System and came to be called the Kalmiopsis Wilderness.

One advantage to hiking the Kalmiopsis is the constant change of scenery. There are deep canyons, rocky ridges, grand vistas, serpentine slopes, crystal clear streams, rivers to fish and play in, and seven small lakes to explore. Because of the extremely rugged terrain, be prepared to do a fair amount of climbing and descending.

The Kalmiopsis Wilderness is often called a "botanists paradise" and with good reason. Recognized as having the largest variety of plant species as any place in Oregon (there are about 1,000 species here), you'll find such rare plants as the pre-ice age shrub the Kalmiopsis leachiana. First discovered near Gold Basin in 1930, the wilderness was later named after this unique treasure. The oldest surviving member of the heath family, the Kalmiopsis flower usually blooms in May or June and resembles a tiny, delicate wild rose, or a miniature rhododendron.

There are other rare species to observe. Look for the Brewer spruce, a rare American spruce, also known as a weeping spruce. Also, there are

Bald eagle.

such beautiful and interesting plants as the rhododendron, azalea, ladys-slipper and the insect-eating California pitcher plant. Please remember that plant collecting is prohibited.

Although black bear, deer, and elk inhabit the wilderness along with many other species of animal and bird life, wildlife populations are not tremendous. The harsh environment found in the Kalmiopsis limits the amount of suitable habitat. Still, if you are lucky you may just see a doe and her fawn tiptoeing into your camp, or maybe you'll see a black bear running across one of the prairies on Bald Mountain.

Mining relics can be seen in many areas of the Kalmiopsis. Drawn to the area in the 1850's, prospectors came to the Kalmiopsis with the dream of cashing in the huge gold nuggets they hoped to find. Nearby towns shot up overnight, they prospered, and later they died. Once old miners' routes, today the trails followed by those with gold fever, are now followed by those trying to gain a sense of peace and serenity found in the Kalmiopsis Wilderness.

There are many advantages to hiking the Kalmiopsis; disadvantages include rattlesnakes, scorpions, and poison oak. Spring and fall are the most pleasant times to visit as the summer months tend to be extremely hot and dry. Those hiking in summer should note which water sources are available year-round.

With a bit of thought and the necessary preparations, a visit to the Kalmiopsis can be a truly rewarding experience. Rare and unusual plants, wildlife, solitude, and rugged wild country combine to make this wilderness the perfect spot for the backpacker who doesn't care for crowds.

PINE FLAT/BALD MOUNTAIN (hike 29)

Trail length: About 13.3 miles one-way. (Includes round-trip side junket to Pine Flat.)

Description: A three-day backpack in the Kalmiopsis Wilderness.

Difficulty: Moderate to strenuous.

Highlights: Creeks and a river; abundant plant life; good fishing; great views. Watch for poison oak and rattlesnakes.

Elevations: 1,000 to 4,000 feet.

Maps: Kalmiopsis Wilderness Map.

California pitcher plant.

Slide Creek Falls.

Hiking season: May through October.

Permits: Trail Park Permit.

Contact: Illinois Valley Ranger District, 26468 Redwood Hwy., Cave Junction, OR 97523; (541) 592-2166.

Directions: Reach the Briggs Creek Trailhead by driving County Road 5070 (Illinois Valley Rd.) from Selma, located off U.S. Highway 199; at 6.7 miles the road turns to Forest Road 4103. Reach the trailhead after 18.3 miles. Although rough in spots, the mostly gravel road is passable in most passenger cars, except those with low clearance.

Trail info: Hike towards Pine Flat by crossing Briggs Creek; after 2.0 miles enter the York Creek Botanical Area. Reach Clear Creek at 4.2 miles. The Forest Service claims Clear Creek may have the clearest water in the world.

At 5.1 miles come to the junction of Pine Flat Trail 1219 and Illinois River Trail 1162. Pine Flat Trail descends 1,000 feet and 0.7 mile to Pine Flat, a grand spot for camping and relaxing.

To reach Bald Mountain, turn right at the junction and continue on the Illinois River Trail, crossing several creeks en route. Reach a fork in the trail at 8.9 miles. The old trail heads off to the right, and the newest trail is on the left. The old trail provides a great view of Chinaman Hat Peak and beyond. But a logging road, cut close to the wilderness boundary, obscures the otherwise beautiful view.

Reach the junction of Florence Way and Bald Mountain at 9.7 miles, coming to Bald Mountain Camp at 11.9 miles.

Bald Mountain Lookout is easy to locate. Just follow the trails up the mountain to the highest point. On a clear day see California's Mt. Shasta, the Klamath Mountains, the Siskiyou Mountains, and the Pacific Ocean.

JOHNSON BUTTE (hike 30)

Trail length: About 7.5 miles one-way.

Description: A long day hike or a two-day backpack in the Kalmiopsis Wilderness.

Difficulty: Moderate; mostly level across the saddle.

Highlights: Rare flowers in the spring; grand views all year. Watch for poison oak and rattlesnakes.

Elevations: 3,200 to 3,920 feet.

Maps: Kalmiopsis Wilderness Map.

Hiking season: Spring and fall; summers are very hot.

Permits: Trail Park Permit.

Contact: Chetco Ranger District, 555 Fifth St., Brookings, OR 97415; (541) 469-2196.

Directions: Drive east on North Bank Road (County Road 784), just south of Brookings off U.S. Highway 101; after 10.6 miles the road changes to Forest Road 1376. Continue another 5.8 miles; turn right on Forest Road 1909 and drive an additional 9.6 miles to a fork. Keep to the left, reaching the trailhead in 5.5 miles.

Trail info: Hike an old mining road, now Johnson Butte Trail 1110, keeping to the left when the trail forks shortly after entering the wilderness. At about 1.4 miles look for a patch of Kalmiopsis leachiana off the trail. Exceedingly rare, the pre-Ice age shrub was first discovered near Gold Basin in 1930. Like a tiny, delicate wild rose (some claim it looks more like a miniature rhododendron), this member of the heath family usually blooms in May or June. Except for a small patch in Oregon's Cascades and four sites just outside the wilderness, it is found almost exclusively within the Kalmiopsis Wilderness.

At 2 miles you'll hike a saddle, with terrific views of your surroundings. Look for more kalmiopsis and other wildflowers as you continue.

Reach a sign for Salamander Lake at 5.2 miles. The lake is just over the ridge and down 300 to 400 feet. Back on the trail, reach a junction near Johnson Butte at 7.5 miles.

VULCAN LAKE (hike 31)

Trail length: About 1.6 miles one-way.

Description: A short day hike in the Kalmiopsis Wilderness.

Difficulty: Easy.

Highlights: Glacier cirque lakes set in serpentine rock; good views; unique plants. Watch for poison oak and rattlesnakes.

Elevations: 3,680 to 4,000 feet.

Maps: Kalmiopsis Wilderness Map.

Hiking season: Spring and fall; summers are very hot.

Permits: Trail Park Permit.

Contact: Chetco Ranger District, 555 Fifth St., Brookings, OR 97415; (541) 469-2196.

Black-crowned night-heron (immature).

Directions: Drive east on North Bank Road (County Road 784), just south of Brookings off U.S. Highway 101; after 10.6 miles the road changes to Forest Road 1376. Continue another 5.8 miles; turn right on Forest Road 1909 and drive an additional 9.6 miles to a fork. Keep to the left, reaching the trailhead in 5.5 miles.

Trail info: Hike an old mining road, now Johnson Butte Trail 1110, keeping to the right on Vulcan Lake Trail 1110A when the trail forks shortly after entering the wilderness. Look for gnarly pines and western azaleas as you hike to a fork in the trail 1.3 miles, just before reaching Vulcan Lake. Turn right and hike 0.1 mile to the lake.

Little Vulcan Lake is close by. To reach it, go back to the main trail, hike an additional 100 yards or so to another fork, and make a right. Descend 0.2 mile to Little Vulcan Lake.

Be sure to observe the Darlingtonia while you are there. Known as the California pitcher plant, these unusual plants trap and digest insects.

Yellow-bellied marmot.

INTRODUCTION TO THE MARK O. HATFIELD WILDERNESS

Waterfalls, waterfalls, and more waterfalls. You'll probably see more waterfalls here, in the Mark O. Hatfield Wilderness, than in any other preserve in the Beaver State. In addition, there are fantastic views into Oregon and Washington from atop mountain peaks and ridges, and wonderful hikes along lush canyons, and a variety of creeks and streams.

Managed by the Mt. Hood National Forest, this popular preserve sits about 30 miles east of Portland and eight miles west of Hood River, Oregon. Comprised of impressive basalt cliffs, hanging meadows, rock outcroppings, broad plateaus, steep talus slopes, lush canyons, waterfalls, lakes, and several high peaks, the wilderness consists of 39,000 acres.

Dedicated in 1984, with the signing of the Oregon Wilderness Act, the lowest point is 1,200 feet, located at several points along the northern boundary. The highest point is 4,736 feet on top of Green Point Mountain.

Originally called the Columbia Wilderness, the preserve was renamed in honor of Senator Mark O. Hatfield. The change was made when President Clinton signed the Appropriation Act of 1997.

One hundred and twenty-five miles of trails crisscross an assortment of habitats. In the west, travel through moss-covered rain forests where Douglas-fir, western hemlock and sword ferns predominant. Scrub oaks dot a semi-arid scabland in the east, a decided difference from the west. The area is so unique that 12 plant species found here are found nowhere else in the world—including six strictly confined to the wilderness lands.

Mt. Adams, Washington from Mt. Defiance Trail.

Crimson columbine.

Rare plants and flowers often grow on north-facing canyons and alpine wildflowers have been known to grow at points near sea level. The colorful beauties are often tricked into doing so. Watch for poison oak below 2,000 feet.

The main drainages—Tanner Creek, Eagle Creek, and Herman Creek—are all oriented in a north-south direction. Several lakes exist as well. An appendage of a Hood River Valley irrigation scheme, those in the east end—Rainy, North, and Bear—were dammed in the early 1900's. Most provide fishing, with native trout found in many area streams and lakes. Some lakes are also stocked with brook trout.

Bird life includes ravens and bald eagles. Forest dwellers consist of gray jays; be sure to look for dippers near waterfalls.

Bear, deer, and the shy cougar inhabit the area, but don't expect to see them unless you're quiet and have the patience to sit still, watching for elusive creatures. Small mammals include chipmunks, pikas, squirrels and shrews.

Trails offering solitude are not easy to find in this heavily-used preserve. Although the Pacific Crest and Eagle Creek Trails are by far the most well-known and used, hikers seeking solitude should concentrate on the less populated trails such Tanner Butte, Herman Creek, Nick Eaton Ridge, and Gorton Creek.

Although portions of the Columbia Gorge are open to hiking most of the year, perhaps the best time for hiking is in early spring when wildflowers paint portions of this land, particularly the open slopes. Late fall is another favorite time as deciduous tree leaves give their last bit of color before falling to the ground.

Precipitation amounts in the west versus the east are just as varied as the land itself. In the west, expect 75 inches, the east receives a mere 29 inches. It's usually dry in summer, but expect hot and humid weather. Winter visitors should have no problem hiking as the lower trails are usually free of snow even in midwinter. Expect wet and cold weather, however. Snow clogs the trails over 3,600 feet in elevation from December to May.

CHINIDERE MOUNTAIN/ TOMLIKE MOUNTAIN LOOP (hike 32)

Trail length: About 7.7 miles for the complete loop.
Description: A day hike in the Mark O. Hatfield Wilderness.
Difficulty: Moderate.
Highlights: Wonderful views; wildflowers.
Elevations: 3,723 to 4,673 feet.
Maps: Columbia/Badger Creek Wilderness Map.
Hiking season: June through October.
Permits: None required.
Contact: Mt. Hood National Forest, 16400 Champion Way, Sandy, OR 97055; (503) 668-1700.
Directions: To reach the trailhead from Zigzag, located off U.S. Highway 26, travel north on paved East Lolo Pass Road (Forest Road 18) for 10.5 miles. At the junction, remain straight on Forest Road 18, traveling a rough road. Continue on Road 18 for 9.9 miles to the junction of Forest Road 13 (Lost Lake Road). Head left, traveling the unsigned road towards Wahtum Lake. At 4.4 miles turn right, now traveling Forest Road 1310 (Scout Lake Road). Reach Wahtum Lake Campground and trailhead in another 5.9 miles.
Trail info: Depart via Wahtum Lake Trail 406H to the Pacific Crest Trail (PCT) junction. At the lake notice the ridge on which you'll return via Anthill Trail. Hike around the east side of the lake via the PCT.

Meet the Herman Creek Trail at 1.7 miles. Turn left, hiking another 0.1 mile to the Chinidere Mountain Trail. Head to the right and climb the steep grade to the summit at 2.2 miles. Wildflowers carpet the peak during early summer, providing a colorful foreground for landmarks Wahtum Lake, Mt. Defiance, Mt. Hood, Tomlike Mountain, Mt. Jefferson and Washington's three giants—Mounts Saint Helens, Rainier and Adams.

To continue the loop head back to the PCT, turn left and hike to Herman Creek Trail 406 at 2.7 miles. Hike another 0.1 mile to a junction, remaining straight on Herman Creek Trail. Reach the junction to Anthill Trail at 3.7 miles. This is your return trail.

Before you leave, travel 50 yards to an unmaintained trail located on a saddle. There isn't much of a trail to Tomlike Mountain, but it's easy to find the summit. For a good view, reach the top of Tomlike Mountain at 4.7 miles.

To continue the loop from the Anthill Trail junction, turn left and climb through the trees to an abandoned road at 6.3 miles. The road leads left to Rainy Lake, right to the PCT. Head straight to Wahtum Lake and descend to the trailhead at 7.7 miles.

Gray jay.

HERMAN CREEK (hike 33)

Trail length: About 7.7 miles one-way.

Description: A day hike or a backpack trip into the Mark O. Hatfield Wilderness.

Difficulty: Moderate to strenuous.

Highlights: Old-growth forest including stately noble firs. This area is recognized as having the best preserve of old-growth trees in the Columbia Gorge Recreation Area.

Elevations: 160 to 2,800 feet.

Maps: Columbia/Badger Creek Wilderness Map.

Hiking season: May through November.

Permits: Trail Park Permit.

Contact: Mt. Hood National Forest, 16400 Champion Way, Sandy, OR 97055; (503) 668-1700.

Directions: To reach the trailhead at the Columbia Gorge Work Center, drive Interstate 84 eastbound to Cascade Locks Exit No. 44, located about 44 miles east of Portland. Drive 1.0 mile through town, going right at the fork towards Interstate 84. Pass under the freeway 0.6 mile from the fork. Turn left at a sign pointing the way to the Oxbow Fish Hatchery and drive 1.7 miles to the work center. Turn right on Forest Road 215, following the signs to the Herman Creek Trailhead at 0.4 mile.

Those going westbound on Interstate 84 should take the Forest Lane-Herman Creek Exit, located three miles east of Cascade Locks. Cross under the freeway, make a right on Forest Lane, then a left on Forest Road 215 in 0.6 mile.

Trail info: As you travel Herman Creek Trail notice the enormous stands of noble firs, western redcedar, western hemlocks and Douglas-firs.

Although Herman Creek Trail extends for 11.2 miles, I spent my time embracing the first 7.7 miles of the trail, hiking to a favorite spot, Cedar Swamp. The trail makes for a good day hike and also works well with other nearby trails in forming some splendid overnight trips.

Watch for poison oak as you begin hiking Herman Creek Trail 406 (actually an old road at this point). Continue to 2.0 miles, a place where the road narrows to a trail and remains so for the duration of this hike.

You won't see Herman Creek until you cross it at 7.6 miles, but you will cross many other streams and creeks as you traverse the Herman Creek drainage. Reach the remains of the Cedar Swamp Shelter at 7.3 miles.

RAINY LAKE/NORTH LAKE LOOP (hike 34)

Trail length: About 7.0 miles for the complete loop.

Description: A day hike in the Mark O. Hatfield Wilderness.

Difficulty: Moderate.

Highlights: Lots of variety on this loop; hike past giant Douglas-fir, delicate ferns; from atop Green Point Ridge gaze down at Rainy Lake, Mt. Hood looming in the near distance.

Elevations: 4,092 to 4,600 feet.

Maps: Columbia/Badger Creek Wilderness Map.

Hiking season: May through October.

Permits: None required.

Contact: Mt. Hood National Forest, 16400 Champion Way, Sandy, OR 97055; (503) 668-1700.

Directions: To reach the trailhead from Zigzag, located off U.S. Highway 26, drive north on paved East Lolo Pass Road (Forest Road 18) for 10.5 miles. At the junction, head straight on Forest Road 18, driving about 10 miles to the junction of Forest Road 13 (Lost Lake Road). Turn right towards Hood River.

Drive 6.1 miles to a junction and head left, continuing on Lost Lake Road. Reach the intersection of Punch Bowl Road after 1.7 miles; keep straight on Punch Bowl Road. Drive 1.4 miles to another junction. Make a right on Forest Road 2820 (Deadpoint Road), a nice gravel road. After 11.0 miles, reach Forest Road 670. Turn right on the unmaintained road, driving 0.1 mile to the Rainy Lake Campground and the trailhead.

Vine maple leaf (in the fall).

Trail info: Hike Rainy Lake Trail 416, reaching 10-acre Rainy Lake in 0.2 mile. Now travel to the right towards North Lake, gradually climbing through the trees to a junction at 0.6 mile. Head straight to Wyeth and North Lake Trails. The trail to the left—Gorton Creek Trail—will be your return.

Hike gradually down and up to Wyeth Trail 411 at 1.5 miles; stay straight. Reach Green Point Ridge Trail 18 at 3.1 miles. Continue along and you'll see a magnificent view of North Lake, Mt. Defiance, Mt. Adams and the Columbia River. Later on there's a spectacular view of Rainy Lake with Mt. Hood in the background.

Back on the trail, descend to a junction at 5.8 miles. Turn left and descend the steep trail to the Rainy Lake junction at 6.4 miles. Head south, hiking past Rainy Lake to the trailhead at 7.0 miles.

INTRODUCTION TO THE MENAGERIE WILDERNESS

Lush forest stretches out across the steep, dissected, slopes of the Menagerie Wilderness. Lofty rock spires and arches—defiant lava intrusions—decorate the solitary landscape. It's a land like no other.

Heavy stands of 125-year-old Douglas fir, western hemlock and western redcedar blanket the area. Vine maple, salal, and sword fern cover most of the forest floor. Here and there, dozens of rock spires reach to the stars, drawing rock climbers from around the Pacific Northwest for technical climbing challenges.

Menagerie's spires are called a "menagerie" of animal names. These include Rabbit Ears, Turkey Monster (a 300-foot pinnacle, unclimbed until 1966), but perhaps the most famous is Rooster Rock. Others include Roosters Tail, Chicken Rock, Hen Rock, the Porpoise, and the Bridge. Two natural arches also grace the area.

Climbing difficulty ranges vary. A class 5.4 skill is required to reach Rooster Rock's abandoned lookout. Three other routes up to the same point range in difficulty to level II-5.8. Big Arch, one of two natural arches, is a level II-5.7-A1 climb. South Rabbit Ear, a 265-foot pinnacle, rates a III 5.7 climb, and North Rabbit Ear rates a III-5.7-A2. Turkey Monster has level III-5.6-A3 and level IV-5.7-A3 routes. The Porpoise rates a I-5.8 and the Bridge a II-5.9.

Climbers and hikers will find four miles of trails penetrating Oregon's smallest wilderness. Located 24 miles east of the small town of Sweet Home, the 5,033-acre preserve ranges in elevation from 1,200 feet along State Highway 20 to 3,900 feet in the northern portion of the region. Managed by the Sweet Home Ranger District of the Willamette National Forest, the area rests on the western side of the Cascade Mountains.

The Forest Service reports that most of the area is used by day hikers, many of them rock climbers. Seventy-five percent reach the interior of

the preserve via the Trout Creek/Rooster Rock trails. (See ROOSTER ROCK and TROUT CREEK for additional details.) Backpackers will find very little flat ground for camping.

Those choosing to backpack anyway, should note that all camps have to be located outside of view and at least 200 feet from any water sources, trails and other key interest features.

The wilderness is open most of the year with year-round access possible from State Highway 20. Snow in the higher elevations usually prohibits access for two to three months during the winter.

Hikers, especially those who are quiet, have the chance to see deer, a questionable amount of elk, grouse and other species as well.

ROOSTER ROCK (hike 35)

Trail length: About 2.1 miles one-way.
Description: A day hike in the Menagerie Wilderness.
Difficulty: Strenuous.
Highlights: Second-growth forest; lush vegetation; impressive rock spires; nice views.
Elevations: 1,280 to 3,567 feet.
Maps: Upper Soda USGS quad.
Hiking season: Most of the year; higher elevations may be covered with snow two to three months of the year.
Permits: Trail Park Permit.
Contact: Sweet Home Ranger District, 3225 Highway 20, Sweet Home, OR 97386; (541) 367-5168.
Directions: Reach the trailhead by traveling east from Sweet Home for 27 miles via U.S. Highway 20. You'll find the marked trailhead a short distance past the entrance to the Fernview Campground.
Trail info: Hike Rooster Rock Trail 3399, traveling through dense vegetation. The trail climbs quickly through a forest of Douglas-fir; reach the Trout Creek Trail junction at 1.6 miles.

Turn right and reach Rooster Rock after a steep climb. Continue to a high point at 2.1 miles. A terrific view of Rooster Rock, the wilderness, and beyond is now possible.

Please note, both this trail and the Trout Creek Trail lead to the same point. Trout Creek Trail is longer, but it's also not as steep. See TROUT CREEK TRAIL for more information.

TROUT CREEK (hike 36)

Trail length: About 3.3 miles one-way.
Description: A day hike in the Menagerie Wilderness.
Difficulty: Moderate.
Highlights: Dense, second-growth forest; ferns and other vegetation; impressive rock spires; nice views.
Elevations: 1,234 to 3,567 feet.
Maps: Upper Soda USGS quad.
Hiking season: Most of the year; higher elevations may be covered with snow two to three months of the year.
Permits: Trail Park Permit.
Contact: Sweet Home Ranger District, 3225 Highway 20, Sweet Home, OR 97386; (541) 367-5168.
Directions: Reach the trailhead, located 70 miles northeast of Eugene, by traveling 24 miles east of Sweet Home via U.S. Highway 20. The trailhead is just past the entrance to the Trout Creek Campground.
Trail info: Hike Trout Creek Trail 3405 through dense vegetation and enter the wilderness in 100 yards. Stay on the well-defined trail when passing several spur trails that are within 0.1 mile of the trail head.

See Rooster Rock through the trees at 2.4 miles; in another 0.4 mile reach a trail junction. The trail to the right leads to the Fernview Campground.

Keep straight at the junction and reach a high point near Rooster Rock, one of many impressive rock spires in the area, at 3.3 miles. From here there's a good view of the wilderness and beyond.

Please note, both this trail and the Rooster Rock Trail lead to the same point. Rooster Rock Trail is shorter, but it's also a lot steeper. See ROOSTER ROCK TRAIL for more information.

INTRODUCTION TO
THE MIDDLE SANTIAM WILDERNESS

One of Oregon's largest, low-elevation, old-growth forests exists here, along with quiet pools, uncrowded trails, and an array of plant and animal life.

The Willamette National Forest manages the Middle Santiam Wilderness, located on the west side of the Cascade Mountains, 56 miles east of Albany. Designated in June, 1984, with the signing of the Oregon Wilderness Act, it is one of Oregon's smallest wilderness areas, but one of the least crowded as well.

Ten miles of trails lead through the 8,542-acre preserve which ranges in elevation from 1,600 feet along the Middle Santiam River to 4,965 feet on top of Chimney Peak.

Wilderness embraces both the north and south sides of the Middle Santiam River. Terrain is steep and rugged, blanketed by forests of Douglas-fir and western hemlock in the lower elevations, shifting to true fir higher up. Look for sugar pine as well. This pine, near it's northern limits here in the Middle Santiam, bears giant cones. Other tree species include western redcedar, and in the wet areas near creeks look for red alder and bigleaf maple.

A 200-foot-high canopy of exceptionally old forest—more than 450 years old—shelters a glorious world of light-pink rhododendrons, lichen-covered snags, delicate wildflowers, and silent pools. Unfortunately, old-growth forests are now rare in Oregon. They provide ideal habitat for many species, however, including 137 vertebrate species, including the controversial spotted owl, and 85 other varieties of birds.

Large mammals exist here, but are often difficult to see. Quiet hikers may observe elk, deer, bear, and beaver. Martins and fishers may live in the area as well. During the winter, elk herds spend their days along the Middle Santiam River and lower Donaca and Swamp Creeks. As the snow recedes in spring, the elegant animals migrate up Swamp Creek to higher ground. This is where the female will calve and the herd will spend the summer.

Donaca Lake—the only lake in the preserve—is popular with campers (approximately 80 percent hike to the lake and no further) and anglers yearning for trout. The three-acre lake supports native cutthroat trout.

If you aren't into fishing, explore the lake and surrounding areas while looking for amphibians such as the Pacific newt, Cascades frog, long-toed salamander, and boreal toad. Other animal species consist of waterfowl including both teal and perhaps America's loveliest duck, the wood duck. Ruffed grouse are commonly seen and you might see a great blue heron fishing the lake as well.

Anglers looking for both rainbow and cutthroat should try the Middle Santiam River. Suckers and Chinook salmon thrive in the Middle Santiam as well. Toppled old-growth trees produce the river's siltfree, gravel-bottomed pools—the spawning sites of a third of the Santiam drainage's Chinook salmon.

Although the river canyon is accessible most of the year, (snow is rare), the higher elevation roads and trails are blocked from snow from December through March or April.

You'll have to wait until spring, summer or fall to visit Chimney Peak, site of a former fire lookout. (See CHIMNEY PEAK TRAIL for more information). From the summit, you'll see the mighty Cascades stretching from Mt. Thielsen in the south to Washington's Mt. Adams in the north. Unfortunately, the closest views are the most disturbing for many unsightly clearcuts mar the land just outside the wilderness boundary.

CHIMNEY ROCK (hike 37)

Trail length: About 9.0 miles one-way.
Description: A very long day hike or a two- to three-day back in the Middle Santiam Wilderness.
Difficulty: Moderate to strenuous.
Highlights: Old-growth forest; solitude; splendid view.
Elevations: 2,300 to 4,965 feet.

Facing page: Rock climber at the Menagerie Wilderness.
Below: Egg Creek, Middle Santiam Wilderness.

Maps: Chimney Peak 7.5-minute USGS quad.

Hiking season: June through October.

Permits: Trail Park Permit.

Contact: Sweet Home Ranger District, 3225 Highway 20, Sweet Home, OR 97386; (541) 367-5168.

Directions: From Sweet Home, go east on U.S. Highway 20. After 25 miles turn left at Upper Soda, traveling Forest Road 2041 (Soda Fork Road). Reach the trailhead in 16.9 miles.

Trail info: Chimney Peak Trail, the only major trail in the preserve, traverses the Middle Santiam Wilderness from east to west, and offers solitude to those who hike here.

Enter the 8,524-acre preserve by hiking Chimney Peak Trail 3382. You'll pass through old-growth western redcedar as you make your way past several creeks, and into a clearcut at 1.2 miles. This area is out of the wilderness.

Head back into the wilderness shortly thereafter, reaching Donaca Lake at 2.8 miles. The trail curves around the northwest end of lake and crosses Egg Creek at 4.3 miles. Several more creeks and streams are crossed before reaching the last one at 7.2 miles.

Around 8 miles the trail steepens, climbing over 600 feet in elevation in less than 1 mile. Old stairs lead toward the summit. The Forest Service doesn't recommend climbing them so if you do so you climb at your own risk. The stairs/steep trail lead to the site of an old lookout where the view is impressive.

INTRODUCTION TO THE MILL CREEK WILDERNESS

Steep ridges and canyons, along with many small streams and lovely meadows form much of Mill Creek Wilderness. In addition, Bingham Prairie, a nearly flat plateau, rests in the northwest corner, and two unique rock outcrops—Twin Pillars and Whistler Point—add to the scenery. Best of all, crowds are few.

Located 20 miles northeast of Prineville, Mill Creek Wilderness was designated as such on June 26, 1984 when President Reagan signed the Oregon Wilderness Act of 1984. Prior to wilderness status the area was classified as a Special Management Area.

Twenty miles of trails lead visitors throughout this 17,400 acre preserve, managed solely by the Ochoco National Forest. Trails include Twin Pillars Trail, a National Recreation Trail since 1979, Belknap Trail, and Wildcat Trail.

The wilderness is located within the southwestern extension of the Blue Mountain Range and is composed of roughly 85 percent mixed conifer forest. The remaining portion is mostly open barren ridge tops. Much of the timber consists of old-growth forest of Douglas-fir and ponderosa pine, with lodgepole pines dominating the northwest corner plateau. While hiking in this area you will undoubtedly notice a lot of dead or dying trees. This is due to an infestation of mountain pine beetles.

The elevation ranges from a low of 3,725 feet along East Fork Mill Creek to a high of 6,240 feet near the view point in the northeast corner of the wilderness. East Fork Mill Creek, a tributary of Ochoco Creek, flows through the center of the preserve, and begins life near the northern portion of the area, then flows southwest through Wildcat Campground.

The best time for hiking Mill Creek is usually from May through October. While higher elevations may experience some lingering snow later in the spring, most of the preserve is usually snowfree by May or June. In the summer, look for highs to be from 75 to 85 degrees with lows in the 40's. Winter temperatures are cold with high and lows ranging from 50 degrees above zero to 15 degrees below zero.

Those interested in snow sports such as cross-country skiing or snowshoeing will find that Mill Creek Road (Forest Road 33) is plowed during the winter months, leading to access at Wildcat Campground. A four-wheel drive vehicle is necessary, though, to get to Forest Road 27 just north of the wilderness.

Spring, summer, and fall visitors will find an abundance of activities to enjoy. There's the chance to do some fishing, look for pretty wildflowers,

Bingham Prairie, Mill Creek Widerness.

Bullfrogs.

day hike, backpack, pan for gold, look for rocks, ride horses, and in the fall, hunting for various game.

Due to the varied terrain, including an abundance of riparian areas, there is a variety of animal life, most of it typical of the Blue Mountain Range. Bird species include pileated woodpeckers and goshawks, American robins, tanagers, and more. Wild turkeys were introduced years ago. Mammals include the rarely seen black bear and mountain lion. Also there are badgers, porcupines, marmots, and the area provides spring, summer, and fall range for deer and elk.

Those who don't care to hike with domestic cattle should be fore-warned that the area receives moderate cattle use from August to October.

And those seeking solitude will want to visit the area anytime except during the fall hunting season when the area becomes quite crowded with hunters.

There are several small surface gemstone claims in the wilderness. Primitive roads lead to four general areas in which the claims are located. These include Whistler Spring-Desolation Canyon, White Rock, Twin Pillars, and Forked Horn Butte. Thundereggs, Oregon's state rock, and agates, are the primary gems mined.

TWIN PILLARS (hike 38)

Trail length: About 5.3 miles one-way.

Description: A long day hike in the Mill Creek Wilderness.

Difficulty: Moderate.

Highlights: Solitude; wildlife; old-growth ponderosa pine forest; unique rock formations.

Elevations: 3,700 to 5,100 feet.

Maps: Mill Creek Wilderness map (available soon).

Hiking season: May through October. Mill Creek Road is plowed during the winter for year-round access.

Permits: None required.

Contact: Prineville Ranger District, 3160 N.E. Third St., Prineville, OR 97754; (541) 416-6500.

Directions: Drive east from Prineville via U.S. Highway 26 for 10.2 miles, then head north on Mill Creek Road for 10.8 miles to the Wildcat Campground. Mill Creek Road becomes Forest Road 33 before reaching the campground, where the trailhead is located.

Trail info: Twin Pillars National Recreation Trail 832 follows along the edge of East Fork Mill Creek then crosses over the road and heads back into the trees before reaching the wilderness in 0.2 mile.

Ford the creek several times as you hike through old-growth ponderosa. A carpet of grasses and wildflowers decorate the forest floor in May and June.

Look for pileated woodpeckers, goshawks, and wild turkeys, three of the many species of birds inhabiting the preserve.

Reach the Twin Pillars area in just over 5 miles. You'll see a sign pointing to the unique rock formation.

INTRODUCTION TO THE MONUMENT ROCK WILDERNESS

Golden eagles soar on high, American kestrels flutter their wings then pounce on mice, and coyotes howl. Elk and deer roam the land, robins flit about, and evening grosbeaks visit campsites. These species, along with grouse, hawks, badgers, bear, and the rare wolverine live in the Monument Rock Wilderness.

Monument Rock Wilderness is located in eastern Oregon, about 30 miles east of John Day. Managed by the Malheur and Wallowa-Whitman National Forests, the area consists of 19,650 acres. Established with the passage of the 1984 Oregon Wilderness Act, 12,620 acres are located in the Malheur National Forest, 7,030 acres in the Wallowa-Whitman National Forest.

Ranging in elevation from 5,120 feet on the Little Malheur River to 7,873 feet atop Bullrun Rock, the area is comprised of ponderosa pine forests in the lower elevations and subalpine species along the higher ridges and peaks. The diverse habitat provides a haven for many animals and plant life as well. Because most of the animals found in the forest are shy and rarely seen, hikers shouldn't expect to view an abundance of wildlife. Of course, it's always nice just knowing that they are there.

From the higher points hikers will view other areas of the wilderness, along with Strawberry Mountain Wilderness to the west. Unfortunately, much of the area surrounding the wilderness has been logged, creating a less-than-pristine view at times.

There are three prominent rocks in the area. Table Rock, located just outside the wilderness, has a fire lookout on top and stretches 7,815 feet into the heavens. Other prominent points include the highest peak,

Ponderosa pine.

Coyote.

Bullrun Rock at 7,873 feet, and Monument Rock, at 7,736 feet, the peak for which the area was named.

Monument Rock Wilderness encompasses the headwaters of the Little Malheur River and the upper drainages of the South Fork of Burnt River as well. Rainbow trout inhabit the Little Malheur River where angling is considered fair to good. Migrating up the river from Beulah Reservoir to spawn, the larger trout swim downstream as the flow diminishes in the summer months.

While hiking the trails, especially along the river drainages, look for dwarf huckleberries. Also, crimson columbine, lupine, and many other species of wildflower and plant life.

A major eyesore in the Monument Rock area is the abundance of cattle grazing in the area. Some of the springs have been fenced to prohibit the bovines from actually stepping in the water, but they are still around, polluting the water, denuding the vegetation, and leaving huge cow piles on the trail. The problem is especially noticeable while hiking the outer sections of the Little Malheur River. If you'd rather not camp with bovines or dodge cow pies all day, the Forest Service recommends visiting the wilderness during the early part of June before the cattle are released in the area.

There are relatively few trails in the area with the two best trails mentioned in this guide. Three other trails are located in the Wallowa-Whitman portion of the wilderness but they are pack trails and they're very steep. The Forest Service recommends these be used for what they were originally intended—pack animals.

LITTLE MALHEUR RIVER (hike 39)

Trail length: About 7.2 miles one-way.
Description: A long day hike or a backpack in the Monument Rock Wilderness.
Difficulty: Moderate.
Highlights: Creeks and rivers, solitude.
Elevations: 5,300 to 6,400 feet.
Maps: Monument Rock Wilderness map.
Hiking season: June through November.
Permits: None required.
Contact: Prairie City Ranger District, P.O. Box 337, Prairie City, OR 97869; (541) 820-3311.
Directions: Reach the Little Malheur Trailhead by driving from Unity, located about midway between John Day and Ontario. Find the junction of U.S. Highway 26 and Forest Road 6005 in the center of town, and head west on Forest Road 6005 for 3.8 miles to a fork in the road. Keep left, staying on Road 6005 for another 3.0 miles to the South Fork Campground and another half mile or so up the road pass the Stevens Creek Campground. Further ahead, pass the Elk Creek Campground. Now you'll see a sign "Rough Rd.—not recommended for vehicles—6 miles" at this point. (Although the road is

rough, passenger vehicles may find it passable if they drive with care.)

Stay to the left at two more forks then reach Forest Road 2652, 9.4 miles from the "rough road" sign. Turn left again, driving 2.0 miles to Elk Flat. Head right on Forest Road 1370, reaching the Little Malheur Trailhead 0.7 mile down the road.
Trail info: Hike south on Little Malheur Trail 366, reaching the Little Malheur River at 2.1 miles. The trail follows the river now, crossing it frequently. You'll reach Bull Run Creek about 4.7 miles.

Hike on, reaching the southern end of the wilderness, the end of the trail, and another trailhead, at 7.2 miles.

MONUMENT ROCK (hike 40)

Trail length: About 2.7 miles one-way.
Description: A day hike in the Monument Rock Wilderness.
Difficulty: Easy.
Highlights: Nice views; wildflowers.
Elevations: 7,455 to 7,736 feet.
Maps: Monument Rock Wilderness map.
Hiking season: June through November.
Permits: None required.
Contact: Prairie City Ranger District, P.O. Box 337, Prairie City, OR 97869; (541) 820-3311.
Directions: Reach the trailhead by driving from Unity, located about midway between John Day and Ontario. Find the junction of U.S. Highway 26 and Forest Road 6005 in the center of town, and head west on Forest Road 6005 for 3.8 miles to a fork in the road. Keep left, staying on Road 6005 for another 3.0 miles to the South Fork Campground and another half mile or so up the road pass the Stevens Creek Campground. Further ahead, pass the Elk Creek Campground. Now you'll see a sign "Rough Rd.—not recommended for vehicles—6 miles" at this point. (Although the road is rough, passenger vehicles may find it passable if they drive with care.)

Stay to the left at two more forks then reach Forest Road 2652, 9.4 miles from the "rough road" sign. Turn left again, driving 2.0 miles to Elk Flat. Proceed left on Forest Road 1370 for 3.6 miles to the trailhead. (For a great view drive 0.7 mile past the trailhead, heading left up the road to the lookout on Table Rock.)
Trail info: From the trailhead, hike down old Forest Road 1370, which is now used as a trail. Reach a trail junction at 0.6 mile. Trail 156 leads to Rock Creek Spring. Continue on Trail 1370 reaching another junction at 1.7 miles. Cross the barbed-wire fence, and go straight and south to another junction at 1.9 miles.

Turn right at the junction and reach Bull Run Spring at 2.2 miles. From this point you can bushwack 0.5 mile south to the top of Monument Rock, 7,736 feet high.

American kestrel falcon (close up of head).

Introduction To The Mt. Hood Wilderness

Oregon's highest peak stands in the heart of the Mt. Hood Wilderness. Stretching 11,237 feet into the heavens, Mt. Hood governs the surrounding preserve, like a queen ruling her country. She rules over a land blessed with dense forest, an abundance of streams, and open ridges where spacious panoramas are possible. In midsummer, a kaleidoscopic of flowers paint many meadows and slopes. Protection for the 73-square-mile, 47,100-acre sanctuary began in 1931. At that time, the Chief of the U.S. Forest Service designated 14,800 acres of Mt. Hood National Forest, naming it the Mt. Hood Primitive Area. In 1940, the area was reduced in size to 14,160 acres and reclassified as a Wild Area. In 1964, the Mt. Hood Wilderness became part of the National Wilderness Preservation System.

Elevations in the wilderness range from 1,800 feet to 11,237 feet atop Mt. Hood. Habitat varies widely with the extreme change in elevation. Timberline stands close to the 6,500-foot level, with thick forests of Douglas-fir blanketing the lower slopes. A rise in elevation brings western hemlock, Pacific silver fir, subalpine fir, noble fir, mountain hemlock and whitebark pine.

The understory is lush and includes huckleberry, vine maple, Oregon grape, salal, devil's club and rhododendron. Vast meadows of blue lupine, penstemon, beargrass, Indian paintbrush, Cascade aster, and western pasque exist. In July, look for parades of white avalanche lilies at Paradise Park. Come August, look for the same at Elk Cove.

Amidst the flowers stands Mt. Hood, a mountain geologists refer to as a stratovolcano, a type of volcano similar to most others in the Cascades range. Experts believe the mountain stopped building in the late Pleistocene Epoch. Once reaching about 12,000 feet, wind, rain, snow, and glaciers wore 800 feet off the crater and much of the north slope over the past centuries.

Known to the Northwest Indians as Wy'East, "a mountain god who spouted flame and hurled boulders skyward," Mt. Hood is composed of lava, mud, and a mixture of loosely consolidated ash, pumice and rock fragments. Mt. Hood is not unlike Mt. Saint Helens which blew it's top in 1980. Stratovolcanoes can grow to substantial stature, but erode more easily. They erupt with the intensity of a bomb.

Miles of trails dissect the preserve, but you won't find any trails leading to the top of Mt. Hood. First climbed in 1857, Mt. Hood's summit has greeted a woman in high heels and a man with no legs. However, Mt. Hood is still a technical climb and should be approached as such. Declaring one of the highest accident rates of any peak in the country, climbers are urged to use extreme caution. The majority of accidents are due to lack of caution and the area's unstable weather patterns. Also, climbers are often ill-equipped. An ice ax, crampons, and rope are essential; experts recommend helmets as well. All climbers must register at the Wy'East Day Lodge at Timberline Lodge.

As in all mountain habitats, the weather is often unpredictable. Summers can be warm, even hot, though nights are sometimes cold. It can snow any month of the year.

Look for numerous species of animal life during your travels. There are at least 15 species of reptiles and amphibians. Bird life includes 150 species and range in size from the smallest hummingbird to the American bald eagle. Forty mammals are known to inhabit the area. Pesky critters include mosquitoes and yellowjackets.

Overcrowding is a serious problem in the wilderness. Camping is off limits in Mt. Hood's meadows as well as the forested "islands" of Elk Meadows and Elk Cove. Where camping is allowed you must camp at least 200 feet from any water source. There's a camping limit of 500 feet or more at well-liked Ramona Falls and a fire restriction of 500 feet at McNeil Point.

Pages 46-47: *Hiker on the Cooper Spur Trail. Mt. Adams and Mt. Rainier in the background. Mt. Hood Wilderness.*
Below: *Mt. Hood, Mt. Hood Wilderness.*

Pacific rhododendron.

COOPER SPUR (hike 41)

Trail length: About 4.0 miles one-way.

Description: A day hike in the Mt. Hood Wilderness.

Difficulty: Moderate to strenuous.

Highlights: Splendid close-up views Mt. Hood and the Newton Clark and Eliot Glaciers.

Elevations: 5,700 to 8,574 feet.

Maps: Mt. Hood Wilderness Map.

Hiking season: July through September.

Permits: Trail Park Permit.

Contact: Zigzag Ranger District, 70220 E. Highway 26, Zigzag, OR 97049; (503) 622-3191.

Directions: Reach the trailhead by driving to the junction of Oregon Highway 35 and Cooper Spur Road, located 22.5 miles south of Hood River and 16.2 miles northeast of Government Camp. Take Cooper Spur Road for 2.3 miles to Forest Road 3512 (Cloud Cap Road). Travel Forest Road 3512 to the trailhead in about 10 miles. The trail begins at the Tilly Jane Campground.

Note that the road leading to the trailhead passes through the Cloud Cap/Tilly Jane Historic District. A brochure, available at a road-side information board, describes how and when the road was made.

Trail info: Begin hiking Tilly Jane Trail 600A, heading left and past the guard station. A sign leads the way past the American Legion Camp at 0.2 mile. At less than a mile, exit the trees and view Mt. Hood and Washington's Mt. Rainier and Mt. Adams.

You'll reach a junction to the Timberline Trail at 1.2 miles. Continue straight up Cooper Spur Trail, past a shelter, eventually switchbacking up the ridge to the end of the trail.

Although it appears as though the 11,237-foot summit would be an easy scramble up the slope, it is not. This is a difficult route and mountaineers need an ice ax, rope, and crampons, when climbing the second most popular climbing route to the summit.

ELK MEADOWS (hike 42)

Trail length: About 6.0 miles for the complete loop.

Description: A day hike in the Mt. Hood Wilderness.

Difficulty: Easy to moderate.

Highlights: Profusion of wildflowers in early summer; nice view of Mt. Hood.

Elevations: 4,470 to 5,280 feet.

Maps: Mt. Hood Wilderness Map.

Hiking season: June through September.

Permits: Trail Park Permit.

Contact: Hood River Ranger District, 6780 Highway 35, Hood River, OR 97041; (541) 352-6002.

Directions: Reach the trailhead by driving to the junction of Oregon Highway 35 and Forest Road 3545, 31.1 miles south of Hood River and 10.6 miles northeast of Government Camp. Turn northwest on Forest Road 3545 (look for sign "Hood River Meadows") and reach the trailhead in 0.4 mile.

Trail info: Hike Elk Meadows Trail 645 to 0.4 mile and the junction to Umbrella Falls Trail 667. Proceed on, crossing a few more creeks before reaching the junction to Newton Creek Trail 646 at 1.0 miles. Stay straight on Elk Meadows Trail.

Just after 2.1 miles come to a four-way junction. Gnarl Ridge Trail heads off to the left, Bluegrass Ridge to the right. (At this point you can hike Bluegrass Ridge Trail 647 to Elk Mountain, then descend back to Elk Meadows. It adds about two miles and 300 feet in elevation gain to this loop.) Keep straight at the junction, reaching the Elk Meadows Perimeter Trail at 2.3 miles. You can hike the loop in either direction as the trail circles the meadow. If the wildflowers are in bloom, look for elephant's head, lupine, asters, paintbrush, buttercup, cinquefoil, marsh marigold, and a lot more.

Reach a junction at 3.0 miles. Elk Meadow Trail continues north from here, ending at the Polallie Trailhead in less than 7 miles. Stay on the loop by hiking the Perimeter Trail around and back to the trailhead.

RAMONA FALLS LOOP (hike 43)

Trail length: About 4.4 miles for the complete loop.

Description: A day hike in the Mt. Hood Wilderness.

Difficulty: Easy.

Highlights: Gorgeous, cascading falls; rhododendrons.

Elevations: 2,800 to 3,500 feet.

Maps: Mt. Hood Wilderness Map.

Hiking season: May through November.

Permits: Trail Park Permit.

Contact: Zigzag Ranger District, 70220 E. Highway 26, Zigzag, OR 97049; (503) 622-3191.

Directions: From Zigzag, located off U.S. Highway 26, turn north on E. Lolo Pass Road, driving 4.1 miles to Forest Road 1825. Cross a bridge over the Sandy River in 0.7 mile. Drive another 1.8 miles to a fork then head left on Forest Road 100; reach another fork in 0.2 mile. Stay straight to the Upper Trailhead which you'll reach in 1.4 miles via a rough road. If you'd rather not drive the road, turn left at the fork, and follow the pavement 0.2 mile to the Lower Trailhead. You'll hike gentle terrain along the Sandy River to the Upper Trailhead in 1.2 miles.

Trail info: Ramona Falls Loop Trail 797 starts by crossing the Sandy River via a large bridge. Reach the junction of the Pacific Crest Trail (PCT) at 2.3 miles. A short distance farther and you'll see and hear magnificent Ramona Falls.

A strict restoration plan is in effect near the falls. Once moss and ferns covered the slope near the falls, but today it is bare dirt, denuded and scared. Please stay behind the railing and do not camp in the vicinity. Camps must be at least 500 feet from the falls.

To complete the loop, hike through a forest of spindly lodgepole pines and other species. Some rhododendrons line the trail and are especially beautiful when they bloom in June.

VISTA RIDGE LOOP (hike 44)

Trail length: About 8.5 miles for the complete loop.

Description: A day hike in the Mt. Hood Wilderness.

Difficulty: Moderate to strenuous.

Highlights: Good view Mt. Hood and its glaciers; lots of glacier fawn or avalanche lilies.

Elevations: 4,460 to 5,920 feet.

Maps: Mt. Hood Wilderness Map.
Hiking season: July through September.
Permits: Trail Park Permit.
Contact: Zigzag Ranger District, 70220 E. Highway 26, Zigzag, OR 97049; (503) 622-3191.
Directions: Reach the trailhead from Hood River by driving Oregon Highway 35 south from the I-84 junction (Exit 64). Go 5.4 miles to Erk Hill Road and make a right. After 1.2 miles turn right on Ehrck Hill Road. (The road changes to "Summit Drive" after you pass the stop sign a short distance ahead.) You'll come to another stop sign in 2.5 miles. Go left on this road. A sign points the way to Lost Lake and the town of Dee. Come to a fork after 4.1 miles: go right then left on Lost Lake Road. There's another fork after 5.1 miles; turn left on Forest Road 13. After 3.0 miles, make a left on Forest Road 18 (Lolo Pass Rd.) There's a fork at 3.3 miles: make a left on Forest Road 16 (Marco Creek Road). Drive another 5.5 miles to a junction. Make a right on Forest Road 1650, a gravel road leading to a fork at 2.8 miles. Go left and up 0.9 mile to the end of the road and trailhead.
Trail info: Hike Vista Ridge Trail 626 to a junction at 0.5 mile; go right to another junction at 2.7 miles.

Directions for a clockwise loop include Eden Park and Cairn Basin. Head left at the junction, traveling the upper reaches of the Wy'East Basin to 3.0 miles. Go right, now traveling the Timberline Trail 600, a trail leading approximately 40 miles around Mt. Hood's base.

Reach Cairn Basin at 3.8 miles and a rock shelter at 4.3 miles. From the shelter walk along the stream to a junction; go straight to Eden Park, hiking Lower Timberline Trail 600H. Reach the outskirts of Eden Park at 4.8 miles.

From the depths of Eden Park, cross several more streams en route to Vista Ridge junction at 5.8 miles. Turn left and head back to the trailhead in 2.7 miles.

YOCUM RIDGE (hike 45)

Trail length: About 7.6 miles one-way.
Description: A long day hike or a backpack in the Mt. Hood Wilderness.
Difficulty: Moderate to strenuous.
Highlights: Wildlife; wildflowers; splendid close-up views of glaciers.
Elevations: 2,800 to 6,200 feet.
Maps: Mt. Hood Wilderness Map.
Hiking season: July through October.
Permits: Trail Park Permit.
Contact: Zigzag Ranger District, 70220 E. Highway 26, Zigzag, OR 97049; (503) 622-3191.
Directions: Reach the trailhead from U.S Highway 26 in Zigzag. From town, go north on East Lolo Pass Road for 4.1 miles. Make a right on Forest Road 1825 and drive 2.5 miles; make a left on Forest Road 100. Continue 1.6 miles to the trailhead.
Trail info: Hike Ramona Falls Loop Trail 797 after crossing the Sandy River. Reach the junction of the Pacific Crest Trail at 1.6 miles. Turn left, reaching Ramona Falls at 2.1 miles.

Look for another junction, the remaining loop trail, just past Ramona Falls. Stay straight on the Pacific Crest Trail; reach a junction at 2.9 miles.

Make a right on Yocum Ridge Trail 771 and hike through dense forest where the forest floor is often covered with rhododendrons. Cross the first of several small seasonal streams at 5.8 miles. If visiting just after snowmelt, you may see thousands of bright yellow avalanche lilies.

At about 6.7 miles you'll see Mt. Jefferson to the south, and there's a terrific view of the Reid Glacier and Sandy River drainage just up ahead.

Reach the end of the trail at 7.6 miles. There's a fantastic view into Sandy Glacier from this point and Mt. Hood, Oregon's highest peak at 11,237 feet, seems close enough to reach out and touch.

INTRODUCTION TO THE MT. JEFFERSON WILDERNESS

It is one of the largest wilderness areas in Oregon, and one of the most popular as well. Wildflowers paint its alpine meadows in early summer, mountain lakes entice anglers, hikers travel through dense forests, across open ridges, over lava fields, and mountain climbers scale its mountains. Needless to say, there's something for everyone in the Mt. Jefferson Wilderness.

It's namesake, Mt. Jefferson, stands guard over the 111,177-acre preserve, roughly 70 miles southeast of Salem and 40 miles northwest of Bend. Straddling both sides of the mighty Cascades, the Willamette, Deschutes, and Mt. Hood National Forests share in managing the area which ranges in elevation from a low of 2,400 feet to 10,497 feet atop Mt. Jefferson, Oregon's second highest peak.

Stands of Douglas-fir, silver fir, subalpine fir, lodgepole pine, mountain hemlock, and several species of cedar cover more than half of the preserve. Brush shrouds an additional 25 percent or so, with vine maple, huckleberry, and rhododendron the most common species.

Beauty such this was first deemed worthy of protection in 1930 when officials established the Mt. Jefferson Primitive Areas. With enactment of the Wilderness Act of 1964, the preserve received wilderness designation.

Nearly 200 miles of trails crisscross this lovely lake-blessed (there are more than 150 lakes) preserve with its steep, talus slopes, lush meadows, placid lakes, rushing streams, and thick forests. The Pacific Crest National Scenic Trail skirts the area for 36 of its 2,600-mile length.

Wildlife watching is always fun; look for deer, bear, elk and coyote. Bald eagles fish in the lakes, grouse scurry across the land. In addition to viewing animals, photography, day hiking, backpacking, photography, and just plain

Park Butte, Mt. Jefferson Wilderness.

Mt. Jefferson, Mt. Jefferson Wilderness.

relaxing, mountain climbing is also popular. Three Fingered Jack and Mt. Jefferson are the most sought-after summits among mountain climbers.

Both peaks are heavily-eroded remnants of what geologists believe to be extinct or possibly dormant volcanoes. Only the central core (the hard lava plug) remains of 7,841-foot Three Fingered Jack; a skirt of subsidiary lava dikes surrounds the core.

Like Three Fingered Jack, a lava spire tops Mt. Jefferson. Unlike its neighbor, however, this is not the mountain's prehistoric plug. Powerful-moving glaciers removed the western third of the mountain, including the original crater. At one time the current summit rock was but a side lava flow. Today, five glaciers grace its slopes.

Named by Meriwether Lewis and William Clark in honor of President Jefferson in 1806, climbers use a dozen routes to scale what many regard as Oregon's most difficult ascent. Crumbling lava makes the climb very difficult, but many find the view from on top worthwhile. Successful climbers see from Washington's Mt. Rainier to California's Mt. Shasta.

Although Three Fingered Jack is much lower and easier to climb, it wasn't scaled until Labor Day, 1923. Climbers have at least five routes to choose from, several of which are highly technical rock climbs.

Like mountain climbing, wildflower viewing is also a popular pastime and probably on the minds of most who enter the wilderness early in the season—usually July—when the mosquitoes are usually dreadful. Most meadows range between 5,000 and 6,000 feet, with Jefferson Park often called the loveliest meadow in the Beaver State.

There's a wide variety of dainty flowers here, with lupine, paintbrush, and heather the most common, but you'll also find hordes of people as well. An estimated 200 to 300 people arrive here on a pleasant summer weekend. Marion Lake sees as many as 500 hikers each weekend. The Eight Lakes Basin receives its share of use, too, with Jorn Lake—the most scenic of the eight—also the most crowded.

In winter, deep snows bring solitude to most areas although cross-country skiers find skiing from the Santiam Pass worthwhile. Snow usually begins falling in October and is often present until late summer.

BOOTH LAKE/PORCUPINE RIDGE LOOP (hike 46)

Trail length: About 21.7 miles for the complete loop.
Description: A backpack trip in the Mt. Jefferson Wilderness.
Difficulty: Moderate to strenuous.
Highlights: Splendid views; scenic lakes; portions of the trail may offer solitude.
Elevations: 4,760 to 6,400 feet.
Maps: Mt. Jefferson Wilderness Map.
Hiking season: July through October.
Permits: Trail Park Permit.
Contact: Sisters Ranger District, P.O. Box 249, Sisters, OR 97759; (541) 549-2111.
Directions: This loop begins at the Santiam Pass Trailhead. Reach it by driving U.S. Highway 20 to the Pacific Crest Trail (PCT) sign, 20.1 miles west of Sisters. Head right (north) and follow the paved road 0.5 mile to the trailhead.
Trail info: Begin hiking north on PCT 2000 to a junction at 0.2 mile. Make a right, hiking an unmarked trail to Square Lake, which you'll reach in 2.0 miles. After 2.2 miles, come to a junction; continue straight to Booth Lake at 3.7 miles. You'll hike out of the wilderness for a brief moment upon reaching 7.7 miles. Continue straight on Old Summit Trail.

You'll head back into the wilderness as you continue, passing the junction to Canyon Creek Meadow, a popular wildflower spot, at 8.1 miles. Reach Wasco Lake at 9.8 miles and follow the trail around the west end of the lake. From here you can take a shortcut up the ridge to the PCT, but you'll miss exploring little Minto Lake at 10.5 miles. Come to a fork in the trail at 10.7 miles and keep left, reaching the PCT junction at 11.2 miles.

Head left on the PCT, passing Catlin Lake at 12.3 miles, and enjoying splendid views along Porcupine Crest as you hike back to the trailhead at 21.7 miles.

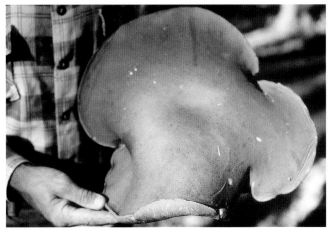

Mushroom, Mt. Jefferson Wilderness.

BINGHAM RIDGE/CATHEDRAL ROCKS (hike 47)

Trail length: About 7.8 miles one-way.
Description: A long day hike or a backpack in the Mt. Jefferson Wilderness.
Difficulty: Moderate to strenuous.
Highlights: Wildflowers; nice views; sometimes solitude.
Elevations: 4,160 to 6,000 feet.
Maps: Mt. Jefferson Wilderness Map.
Hiking season: July through October.
Permits: Trail Park Permit.
Contact: Detroit Ranger District, HC 73, Box 320, Mill City, OR 97360; (503) 854-3366.
Directions: From Idanha, drive southeast on Oregon Highway 22, for 10.5 miles; make a left (go east) on Forest Road 2253, driving 5.5 miles to the trailhead.
Trail info: Bingham Ridge Trail 3421 begins in a clearcut, but enters the forest soon after. The trail ends and comes to a T-junction in 3.4 miles; go left on Lake of the Woods Trail 3493 for 4.6 miles to an unnamed lake where hikers may want to look for flickers, grouse, and other species.

Pass Papoose Lake and a small pond before reaching a junction at 5.9 miles. Go right on Trail 3440 (a sign points the way to the Pacific Crest Trail), crossing a couple of huge rock slides where pikas may whistle a warning.

Farther along you'll look 800 feet below to Hunts Cove, a lush basin of lakes and streams. See Cathedral Rocks to the east. For a closer view hike to 7.8 miles and the Pacific Crest Trail junction. From here, stunted hemlock and dainty wildflowers adorn lava slopes, make a fitting foreground for the rugged Cathedral Rocks and Mount Jefferson seen in the background.

JEFFERSON PARK (hike 48)

Trail length: About 6.5 miles one-way.
Description: A long day hike in the Mt. Jefferson Wilderness.
Difficulty: Moderate to strenuous.
Highlights: Wildflowers; numerous tarns, streams and creeks, alpine lakes; grand scenes.
Elevations: 3,340 to 6,000 feet.
Maps: Mt. Jefferson Wilderness Map.
Hiking season: July through October.
Permits: Trail Park Permit.
Contact: Detroit Ranger District, HC 73, Box 320, Mill City, OR 97360; (503) 854-3366.
Directions: From the junction of Oregon Highway 22 and Forest Road 46 in Detroit, go northeast on Road 46 for 11.5 miles. Make a right on Forest Road 4685; continue 4.8 miles to the trailhead.
Trail info: Several trails lead to Jefferson Park, but the one listed here— South Breitenbush Trail 3375—is the least crowded.

Hike Trail 3375 through the forest and across semi-open slope to a junction at 1.9 miles; continue straight towards the Pacific Crest Trail (PCT).

You'll encounter creeks, tarns, and meadows as you continue your journey to 5.1 miles and the northwest portion of Jefferson Park. Here you'll find meadows, ponds, springs, flowers, and water water everywhere.

At 5.7 miles you'll be close to the South Breitenbush River, which you'll cross at 6.0 miles. The trail splits immediately after wards. To continue to the PCT, go left past several tarns to 6.5 miles and the PCT junction. Jefferson Park is easily explored from this point.

PYRAMID BUTTE (hike 49)

Trail length: About 1.6 miles one-way.
Description: A day hike in the Mt. Jefferson Wilderness.
Difficulty: Moderate.
Highlights: Spectacular views; lush meadows.
Elevations: 5,500 to 6,095 feet.
Maps: Mt. Jefferson Wilderness Map.
Hiking season: July through mid-September.
Permits: Trail Park Permit.
Contact: Estacada Ranger District, 595 NW Industrial Way, Estacada, OR 97023; (503) 630-4256.
Directions: From the junction of Oregon Highway 22 and Forest Road 46 in Detroit, drive northeast on Forest Road 46 for 16.5 miles. Go right on Forest Road 4220, also called "Skyline Road," for 6.6 miles to the trailhead where you'll see a sign "PCT-South."
Trail info: Hike south on the Pacific Crest Trail (PCT) 2000, ignoring the side trails leading to Breitenbush Lake. You may see signs saying this is the Oregon Skyline Trail. The trail was later rerouted and renamed the PCT.

Reach an old sign "Oregon Skyline Trail" and a junction at 1.1 miles. Head north and up Pyramid Butte. Reach the top at 1.6 miles.

Atop the summit—where the remains of an old fire lookout are visible—you'll see Mt. Hood, Olallie Butte, and Olallie Lake in the distant north. Breitenbush Lake and Ruddy Hill are nearby to the northeast and north. If you climb the boulders to the south you'll see Mt. Jefferson and other wilderness highlights.

TRIANGULATION PEAK (hike 50)

Trail length: About 2.3 miles one-way.
Description: A day hike in the Mt. Jefferson Wilderness.
Difficulty: Easy.
Highlights: Wonderful views; little-used trail is perfect for the whole family.
Elevations: 4,800 to 5,434 feet.

Three Fingered Jack, Mt. Jefferson Wilderness.

Maps: Mt. Jefferson Wilderness Map.
Hiking season: July through October.
Permits: Trail Park Permit.
Contact: Detroit Ranger District, HC 73, Box 320, Mill City, OR 97360; (503) 854-3366.
Directions: From Idanha, drive east on Oregon Highway 22 for 1.7 miles; make a left (go north) on Forest Road 2233 (McCoy Creek Road) and travel another 9.2 miles to the trailhead. The trailhead is on the right, at the junction of Forest Roads 2233 and 635. A sign points the way.
Trail info: Hike Triangulation Trail 3373 through trees and lush vegetation to 1.3 miles. Here, there's a good view of Spire Rock. Reach the junction of Triangulation Peak Trail 3374 at 1.6 miles. Head to the right to the summit and site of an old lookout at 2.3 miles.

The view from atop Triangulation Peak is outstanding, especially if you can steer your eyes away from the ugly clearcuts that mar much of the area. Look straight to the north and you'll see beyond Mt. Hood to some of Washington's giants. To the south see Three Fingered Jack, Mt. Washington, and the Three Sisters. Look farther and you'll view Diamond Peak's gentle summit. Mt. Jefferson and much of the wilderness is easily viewed to the east and you'll see an ocean of mountain ridges and valleys to the west.

INTRODUCTION TO THE MT. THIELSEN WILDERNESS

The Mt. Thielsen Wilderness is a combination of mountain peaks and streams, deep blue lakes, a rushing river, wildflowers and wildlife, majestic beauty, and more.

Hikers making their way up Cottonwood Creek, an area where trails do not exist, find solitude and little evidence of man's existence. In contrast, from high atop Mt. Thielsen, hikers can view the surrounding wilderness and the mountains and valleys beyond.

Located directly north of Crater Lake National Park, the wilderness is situated along the crest of the Cascade Mountains and ranges in elevation from a low of 4300 feet along the Umpqua River to a high of 9,182 feet atop Mt. Thielsen. Located within the 157,000-acre Oregon Cascade Recreation Area, the 55,100-acre preserve contains 78 miles of hiking trails, including 26 miles of the Pacific Crest Trail (PCT) which traverses the full length of the wilderness from a point near Summit Rock to Tolo Mountain.

Three agencies—The Winema, Umpqua, and Deschutes National Forests—manage the preserve, designated as such by the Oregon Wilderness Act of 1984.

Mt. Thielsen often reminds travelers of Switzerlands' Matterhorn. Certainly the most prominent peak in the wilderness, the mountain most likely began erupting during the late Pliocene Epoch, producing liquid streams of basalt. During the many thousands of years that followed, these streams combined to form an extensive, gently-sloping shield, not unlike a monstrous, inverted satellite television dish.

With a base 11 miles in diameter, and a crater more than a mile and half across, the shield reached to a height of some 5000 to 6000 feet. And because the shield was flat-topped, its slopes reached an angle of only five degrees.

Mt. Thielsen's height was increased to perhaps 10,000 feet as a large pyroclastic cone developed within its summit crater, ultimately filling, then spilling over the brim of the crater and down its sides.

Today, the upper portion of Mt. Thielsen is like a church steeple, its peak a tower standing above the main structure below. The combined forces of erosion and glacier activity stripped away the loose pyroclastic material surrounding the plugs and dikes, exposing what was once the inner mountain.

Mt. Thielsen is often called "the lightning rod of the Cascades." Named about 1872, in honor of Hans Thielsen, a prominent railroad engineer and builder, its Matterhorn-like spire attracts countless lightning

Cottonwood Creek, Mt. Thielsen Wilderness.

Mt. Thielsen, Mt. Thielsen Wilderness.

National Park and east of Diamond Lake. From the junction of Oregon Highway 138 and Oregon Highway 230 junction, drive north 1.5 miles via Oregon Highway 138 to the trailhead which is on the right (east) side of the road.

Trail info: Mt. Thielsen Trail 1456 climbs to the junction of the Pacific Crest Trail at 3.9 miles. Known as the PCT, it heads northeast and southeast, while there's an unmaintained trail dissecting the two and leading up the ridge to the summit. Take the unmaintained trail. From this point on, there are terrific views of the glaciated features of this high Cascade peak. Use caution as you ascend for the mountain crumbles as you climb. If you're climbing below someone else, please stay off to one side and watch for falling rocks.

It's a 1,700 foot climb from the PCT junction to the scariest point of the entire journey. About 80 feet below the summit you'll have to make the decision whether to continue or just enjoy the view (which is superb) from this particular spot. Although some folks choose to use ropes for the what-seems-like-a-near-vertical-climb-to-the-summit, others just use care, following faint yellow paint marks to the summit. (The choice is yours, but everyone I've talked with advises that you use ropes. One rock climber used the old cliche to make his point: "Better to be safe than sorry.")

From the summit, you'll see Crater Lake, Mt. McLoughlin, Mt. Shasta, Diamond Peak, the Three Sisters, and on a clear day Oregon's highest peak, Mt. Hood, is visible.

TENAS PEAK (hike 52)

Trail length: About 11.6 miles one-way.
Description: A backpack trip in the Mt. Thielsen Wilderness.
Difficulty: Moderate.
Highlights: Great views.
Elevations: 5,640 to 6,750 feet.
Maps: Mt. Thielsen Wilderness Map.
Hiking season: July through September.
Permits: None required.
Contact: Chemult Ranger District, P.O. Box 150, Chemult, OR 97731; (541) 365-7001.
Directions: Reach the Miller Lake Trailhead by driving just north from

bolts. (For those wishing to climb to the summit, you'll find an unmaintained trail leading from the southeast side to a point near the summit. From this point on some climbers use a safety line, others do not. The Forest Service recommends that you do.)

Anglers can cast their lines into both Maidu Lake and Lake Lucile, the only lakes located within the wilderness. The North Umpqua River, Evening Creek, and Little Deschutes River support the only other fisheries in the area.

Plant lovers should delight in the array of plants found in the alpine, sub-alpine, and coniferous forest zones. Wildflower enthusiasts may find the Cascade daisy, and Suksdorf's campion, both sensitive plants believed to occur in the area.

Wildlife abounds too, although it's not so easy to observe. Quiet hikers may see deer, elk, or bear, also pine marten, fisher, badger, fox, and wolverine.

Bird life includes the Clark's nutcracker, common raven, Oregon junco, gray jay, red-tailed hawk, ruffed grouse and blue grouse. In addition, a peregrine falcon has been sighted from the top of Mt. Thielsen, and our national bird, the American bald eagle, has been sighted at Maidu lake. Backpackers will want to explore during the summer months when the days are pleasant, the nights cool. Be prepared for rain or snow anytime of year. As in many high mountain areas you're bound to be tormented by mosquitoes just after snow melt. For a more enjoyable visit hike in July or later and be sure to bring insect repellent. Or visit in winter and ski to your heart's content.

MT. THIELSEN (hike 51)

Trail length: About 5.0 miles one-way.
Description: A long day hike in the Mt. Thielsen Wilderness.
Difficulty: Moderate to strenuous.
Highlights: Terrific views.
Elevations: 5,360 to 9,182 feet.
Maps: Mt. Thielsen Wilderness Map.
Hiking season: July through September.
Permits: None required..
Contact: Diamond Lake Ranger District, HC 60/Box 101, Idleyld Park, OR 97447; (541) 498-2531.
Directions: The trailhead is located just a few miles north of Crater Lake

Hikers admire Diamond Lake from atop Mt. Thielsen.

Hiker at Mt. Thielson Wilderness Area.

Chemult via U.S. Highway 97. Turn left on Forest Road 9772 and follow it about 13 miles to Miller Lake. The trailhead is at the day use area of the Digit Campground.

Trail info: Hike Miller Lake Trail 3725A along the northwest side of the lake. At 0.8 mile reach a sign, "Miller Lake Recreation Area"; make a left. At 2.7 miles reach the junction of the Miller Lake Trail and the Pacific Crest Trail (PCT).

Turn right at the junction, eventually walking a ridge where there are wonderful views. Reach Tolo Camp, located on a wooded saddle, at 8.5 miles. From here, you'll descend then climb across the slope of Tolo Mountain. Reach the junction of the PCT and Tolo Creek Trail 1466 at 10.5 miles. Turn left and descend to the junction of Tenas Peak Trail at 11.1 miles. The Tolo Creek Trail continues to Kelsay Valley trail - 6.5 miles away. Take Tenas Peak Trail 1445 and climb around to the south side of Tenas Peak, then up for a magnificent view of the surrounding wilderness and beyond.

TIPSOO PEAK (hike 53)

Trail length: About 3.2 miles one-way.
Description: A day hike in the Mt. Thielsen Wilderness.
Difficulty: Easy to moderate.
Highlights: Spectacular views; wildlife; wildflowers.
Elevations: 6,500 to 8,034 feet.
Maps: Mt. Thielsen Wilderness Map.
Hiking season: Mid-June through October.
Permits: None required..
Contact: Diamond Lake Ranger District, HC 60/Box 101, Idleyld Park, OR 97447; (541) 498-2531.
Directions: From the junction of Oregon Highways 138 and 230, just south of Diamond Lake Recreation Area and 3.1 miles north of the north entrance to Crater Lake National Park, drive 8.2 miles north on Oregon 138. Make a right on Forest Road 4793 (Cinnamon Butte Road), traveling 1.7 miles to a fork; Forest Road 4793 heads off to the left. Continue straight on Forest Road 4793-100 (Wits End Road), which leads to the trailhead in another 3.5 miles.
Trail info: Hike Tipsoo Trail 1472 to 2.7 miles where there are wonderful views of Mt. Baily and Mt. Thielsen. (See MT. THIELSEN for more information.)

After a total of 3.2 miles reach the summit, a jumble of red, knife-sharp lava rocks, and stunted whitebark and lodgepole pines.

INTRODUCTION TO THE MT. WASHINGTON WILDERNESS

It's always nice to find a place where you can actually see nature at work. It seems as though we often forget about Mother Nature once the land beneath is covered with forests, farm fields, cities, and roads. We go about our daily business, rarely thinking of the role life's forces has entertained upon the earth on which we work and play.

Visit the Mt. Washington Wilderness, and you'll see that Mother Nature has indeed been hard at work. Hardened lava flows blanket much of the preserve, so much so that it is often called the "Black Wilderness."

If you like lava—enjoy it's rugged sharp texture, like to imagine watching the flows of long ago—then you're in luck when venturing to this part of the Beaver State. You'll find 75 square miles of jagged lava flows to explore. But this 52,738-acre sanctuary is much more than lava. There are mountain forests to hike and camp in, tall peaks—including the piercing point of Mt. Washington—to climb, and clear blue lakes to swim and fish in.

Located 70 miles east of Eugene and 31 miles west of Bend, the preserve stretches in elevation from a low of 3,000 feet near the western boundary, to 7,794 feet atop Mt. Washington. Spreading out across the Cascade Crest, the wilderness is a mixed bag of mountain hemlock, true fir, lodgepole pine, and ponderosa pine.

Managed by the Deschutes and Willamette National Forests, this area was first protected as a Wild Area in 1957. In 1964, the Mt. Washington Wild Area became one of the first units of the newly created National Wilderness Preservation System.

Typical of numerous Cascade volcanoes, Mt. Washington developed during the Pleistocene Time (Ice Age) about two million years ago. Once a broad shield-shaped volcano, glacier activity wore the huge mountain down to little more than the original plug. In other words, what you see today.

Hikers will find plenty of recent volcanic activity in the surrounding area. In fact, this area is more active volcanically than other parts of the Oregon Cascades. User trails lead to the summits of both Mt. Washington and Belknap Crater, a cinder-and-ash cone with three distinct craters. A maintained trail leads to Little Belknap where you'll see excellent examples of volcanic spatter-cones, with conduits embracing both lava stalactites and stalagmites.

Lava must have proven a problem for early travelers, but their determination proved tougher. An early Indian trail crosses south of the present-day McKenzie Pass. In 1860, the first route used by white men was opened by Felix Scott, Jr. and his party. In 1872, the McKenzie, Salt Springs and Deschutes Wagon Road Company completed a toll road over much of the present highway. The original road was covered with gravel in 1925 and paved in the early 1930's. Today, it's possible to see some of the original road, skirting the lava, near the Dee Wright Observatory.

Animal life is abundant here. Look for black-tailed deer, mule deer, elk, black bear, and cougar. Small mammals include marmot, ground squirrel, pine marten, pika, coyote, fox and snowshoe rabbit. Birds consist of ruffed and blue grouse, and a whole lot more.

Mountaineers travel up Mt. Washington's eroded lava plug all summer long. Technical climbs include the North Ridge route, the first route climbed. A couple of different ratings are listed for the route; both level I-4.0 and level I-5.1. A dozen more climbing routes increase in difficulty with a level III-5.7 on the east face and a level II-5.8, Chimney of Space, on the west. Although some choose to climb without ropes or other equipment, the Forest Service suggests treating this as a technical climb. Rotten rock makes climbing without proper equipment even more dangerous.

Summers in the Mt. Washington Wilderness are usually warm and dry; winters are cold. McKenzie Pass closes with the first big snow, sometime in November or December and opens again in May or June. Mosquitos are atrocious early in the season; hikers should wait until August or nordic ski in the winter. Santiam Pass provides year-round access.

MT. WASHINGTON'S PACIFIC CREST TRAIL (PCT)
(hike 54)

Trail length: About 13.0 miles one-way.
Description: A backpack trip in the Mt. Washington Wilderness.
Difficulty: Moderate to strenuous.
Highlights: Abundant wildlife and wildflowers; massive lava flows; spectacular views.
Elevations: 4,644 to 6,305 feet.
Maps: Mt. Washington Wilderness Map.
Hiking season: July through October.
Permits: Trail Park Permit.
Contact: McKenzie Ranger District, State Highway 126, McKenzie Bridge, OR 97413; (541) 822-3381 or Sisters Ranger District, P.O. Box 249, Sisters, OR 97759; (541) 549-2111.
Directions: Reach the northern PCT trailhead, which is near Big Lake, by driving U.S. Highway 20 to Big Lake Road (Forest Road 2690), located 21 miles west of Sisters. Travel south for 3.2 miles, then left on Forest Road 811 for 0.5 mile to the marked trailhead.

The southern PCT trailhead at McKenzie Pass is off Oregon Highway 242, 15 miles west of Sisters, 26 miles east of McKenzie Bridge. The road is closed during the winter months; check with the Forest Service for opening dates.
Trail info: About 13 miles of the Pacific Crest Trail, a 2600-mile, Mexico-to-Canada trail, traverses the Mt. Washington Wilderness. It's a perfect hike for those with a shuttle available. If you begin at the south end (McKenzie Pass) and have a shuttle waiting at the north end (Big Lake), you'll save yourself about 600 feet of climbing. However, this text begins in the north.

From the trailhead near Big Lake, go south on PCT Trail 2000. At 2.9 miles there's a rock cairn and orange flag; this unmaintained trail leads to Mt. Washington, which is a technical climb and should not be attempted unless you have the proper gear and experience. The rock on the mountain crumbles easily.

You'll pass through enormous lava flows upon reaching the Little Belknap Crater junction at 10.6 miles. There's a 0.2 mile trail leading to a 360-degree view of the surrounding area. It is a must-see.

PATJENS LAKE LOOP (hike 55)

Trail length: About 5.8 miles for the complete loop.
Description: A day hike in the Mt. Washington Wilderness.
Difficulty: Moderate.
Highlights: Pretty lake; wildflowers.
Elevations: 4,688 to 4,800 feet.
Maps: Mt. Washington Wilderness Map.
Hiking season: July through October.
Permits: Trail Park Permit.
Contact: McKenzie Ranger District, State Highway 126, McKenzie Bridge, OR 97413; (541) 822-3381.
Directions: Reach the trailhead at Big Lake, 21 miles west of Sisters, by driving U.S. Highway 20 to Big Lake Road (Forest Road 2690). Travel south and reach the Big Lake Campground after 3.6 miles. If you're just interested in a day hike, or you'd rather camp at Patjens Lakes, keep straight instead of entering the campground, and reach the trail head in another 0.6 mile.
Trail info: From the trailhead hike 0.1 mile to the Patjens Lake Trail 3395 junction. Head either way to complete the loop; this guide describes the loop counterclockwise.

Reach a trail leading right to the Cayuse Horse Camp at 1.3 miles. You'll come to a crest at 1.7 miles; peer through the trees for a view of Mt. Washington and the Three Sisters. An unnamed lake is on the south side of the trail at 2.5 miles; come to the first of three Patjens Lakes at 3.0 miles. The largest of the lakes is at 3.4 miles; the third is accessible at 3.6 miles.

Upon reaching 4.7 miles you'll see a well-defined spur trail leading to the Pacific Crest Trail, about 0.2 mile to the east. At 5.0 miles reach an unmaintained trail, this one leads around Big Lake

Hand Lake, Mt. Washington Wilderness.

Patjens Lake, Mt. Washington Wilderness.

INTRODUCTION TO
THE MOUNTAIN LAKES WILDERNESS

Mountain Lakes Wilderness has something for everyone. There are clear lakes, lofty mountains, good fishing, abundant animal life, and much more.

Several million years ago a 12,000 foot massive composite volcano was "born" in the area which is now the wilderness. The huge volcano covered roughly 85 square miles, making it one of the giants of the southern Cascades.

The mountain lost its status as "one of the giants," however, when the summit portion of the volcano collapsed into a huge crater or caldera. The same volcanic forces that once formed the mountain were now responsible for destroying it.

Later the earth cooled. Snow and ice gathered in the caldera depths, forming glaciers which spilled over the rim and spread slowly down the sides of the mountain. Time passed. The caldera was reshaped as repeated glaciation combined with wind and water to tear at the mountain, leaving only fragments of the rim and portions of the base.

Mountain Lakes was first established as a primitive area in 1930 when the National Forest Service set aside 13,444 acres. In 1940 Mountain Lakes was increased to its present size—23,071 acres—and the area was renamed the Mountain Lakes Wild Area. With the passage of the Wilderness Act of 1964 the area was once again renamed and Mountain Lakes Wilderness became a segment of the National Wilderness system.

The preserve, managed by the Winema National Forest, is 15 airline miles northwest of Klamath Falls and 40 airline miles south of Crater Lake National Park. Most of the wilderness lies above 6,000 feet, with Aspen Butte claiming the highest point at 8,208 feet.

There are three trails—Varney Creek, Mountain Lakes, and Clover Creek—leading into the wilderness. All three trails lead to the primary trail—Mountain Lakes Loop Trail —which traces a nine-plus mile loop around the ancient caldera rim.

Great horned owl (adult).

which is due south. Head left, traveling around the west end of the lake. Proceed to another junction at 5.5 miles; both trails lead to the trailhead.

SCOTT MOUNTAIN (hike 56)

Trail length: About 4.0 miles one-way.
Description: A day hike in the Mt. Washington Wilderness.
Difficulty: Moderate to strenuous.
Highlights: Spectacular views.
Elevations: 4,800 to 6,116 feet.
Maps: Mt. Washington Wilderness Map.
Hiking season: July through October.
Permits: Trail Park Permit.
Contact: McKenzie Ranger District, State Highway 126, McKenzie Bridge, OR 97413; (541) 822-3381.
Directions: From McKenzie Bridge, travel east on Oregon Highway 126. Reach the junction of Oregon Highway 242 at 4.8 miles; turn right on Oregon 242, which is closed during the winter. Check with the Forest Service for opening dates (usually June or July). Drive 15.9 miles to Forest Road 260; make a left, going 0.9 mile to the trailhead at Scott Lake.
Trail info: Hike Benson Trail 3502, traveling through the forest to Benson Lake at 1.3 miles. Pass a series of ponds as you head to a spur trail leading to Tenas Lakes at 2.5 miles. A 0.1 mile trail leads to the largest of seven rock-lined lakes.

Reach an unmarked junction near 3.7 miles; stay left and hike in awe of Oregon's five highest peaks: Mount Jefferson, Mount Hood, and the Three Sisters—North, Middle and South.

Below 7,000 feet the trails wind through heavy stands of mountain hemlock mixed with Shasta red fir. At higher elevations the mountains are rich with alpine fir, white pine, and lodgepole pine. An occasional mountain meadow may also be found, particularly in the lower basins. During the spring and summer months brilliant wildflowers emerge to brighten the lengthening days of summer.

Mountain lakes are plentiful with the majority of lakes found along the rim of the old crater. These lakes range in size from small ponds to larger lakes like Lake Harriette. With a surface of 70 acres, Lake Harriette is not only the largest lake in the wilderness, but also the deepest. Its refreshing, blue waters reach a depth of 63 feet.

A variety of mammals, such as deer, bear, coyote, and bobcat live in the area. A wide variety of birds are commonly seen too, including bald eagles, osprey, owls, hawks, and numerous forest dwelling birds, like jays and nuthatches.

After snowmelt a few unpleasant creatures invade the area. Mosquitoes, gnats, and black flies can be expected in the early part of the season. After July, bugs are usually not a problem but carry insect repellent just in case.

As in all mountainous regions, the weather is always unpredictable. Frost can occur on any night throughout the summer and sudden thunderstorms are frequent in July and August. During the winter, temperatures are very cold and snow accumulates to a depth of eight to 15 feet or more.

During the summer months the trails are used by day hikers, backpackers, and people on horseback. But Mountain Lakes is also a great spot for winter sports. Snowshoers and cross-country skiers will enjoy the beauty and peace found on a crisp, winter day. Winter travelers should be aware of the elements and winter survival techniques before entering the wilderness.

ASPEN BUTTE (hike 57)

Trail length: About 6.3 miles one-way.
Description: A long day hike or a backpack trip in the Mountain Lakes Wilderness.

Soft arnica.

Lake Harriette, Mountain Lakes Wilderness.

Difficulty: Moderate to strenuous.
Highlights: Wildflowers; lovely creek; spectacular views.
Elevations: 5,720 to 8,208 feet.
Maps: Mountain Lakes Wilderness Map.
Hiking season: Mid-June through late October.
Permits: None required.
Contact: Klamath Ranger District, 1936 California Ave., Klamath Falls, OR 97601; (541) 885-3400.
Directions: From the triple junction—U.S. Highway 97, Oregon 140 and Oregon 66—just south of Klamath Falls, head southwest on Oregon 66 toward Keno. After 8.7 miles, turn right on Clover Creek Road and continue another 16.3 miles; make a right on Forest Road 3852, and drive to the end of the road and trailhead in another 3.4 miles.
Trail info: Hike Clover Creek Trail 3722 to Clover Creek at 0.6 mile and then continue upstream, hiking parallel to the creek. Farther up the trail you'll pass a number of small lakes (note that most of the lakes are farther off the trail), all part of the Clover Lake group, an assembly of 36 small lakes.

Reach Mountain Lakes Loop Trail 3727 after hiking 3.1 miles; stay to the right. As you continue, you'll hike near the rim of the caldera upon reaching the 4.4-miles mark.

You'll reach the junction to Aspen Butte after traveling 5.1 miles from the trailhead. Head south up the unmaintained, but signed trail, watching for tree blazes as you climb. Although portions of the trail are unmarked, the summit is easy to find. Your reward is a 360-degree view of California's Mt. Shasta, Upper Klamath Lake, Oregon's largest body of water, and Mt. McLoughlin, southern Oregon's highest peak.

MOUNTAIN LAKES LOOP (hike 58)

Trail length: About 16.5 miles for the complete loop.

Description: A super-long day hike, or a backpack trip in the Mountain Lakes Wilderness.

Difficulty: Moderate to strenuous.

Highlights: Wildflowers; lovely creek and lakes.

Elevations: 5,720 to 7,520 feet.

Maps: Mountain Lakes Wilderness Map.

Hiking season: Mid-June through late October.

Permits: None required.

Contact: Klamath Ranger District, 1936 California Ave., Klamath Falls, OR 97601; (541) 885-3400.

Directions: From the triple junction—U.S. Highway 97, Oregon 140 and Oregon 66—just south of Klamath Falls, head southwest on Oregon 66 toward Keno. After 8.7 miles, turn right on Clover Creek Road and continue another 16.3 miles; make a right on Forest Road 3852, and drive to the end of the road and trailhead in another 3.4 miles.

Trail info: Hike Clover Creek Trail 3722 to Clover Creek at 0.6 mile and then continue upstream, hiking parallel to the creek. Farther up the trail you'll pass a number of small lakes (note that most of the lakes are farther off the trail), all part of the Clover Lake group, an assembly of 36 small lakes.

Reach Mountain Lakes Loop Trail 3727 after hiking 3.1 miles; stay to the right if you're hiking in a counterclockwise fashion.

You'll reach the junction to Aspen Butte after traveling 5.1 miles from the trailhead. (See ASPEN BUTTE for more information.) As you continue you'll pass several lakes, including Lake Harriette. Bald eagles and osprey are often seen in the area.

Reach the Mountain Lakes Loop Trail/Clover Creek Trail junction at 13.4 miles. Reach the trailhead after a total of 16.5 miles.

INTRODUCTION TO THE NORTH FORK JOHN DAY WILDERNESS

The North Fork John Day Wilderness is a land of diversity. There are the high, craggy, granite peaks, the rugged gorge of the North Fork John Day River, and an abundance of wildlife. Known for its big game population of Rocky Mountain elk and mule deer, the area is also a superb fish habitat. The main stem of the North Fork John Day River and its tributaries provide approximately 40 miles of superior quality spawning for anadromous and resident fish.

Located in the Blue Mountain Range, the wilderness includes portions of the Elkhorn and Greenhorn Mountains. Three National

Rocky mountain elk (close up of bull).

Red-tailed hawk (adult).

Recreation Trails—Elkhorn Crest, North Fork John Day, and Winom Creek—meander through the wilderness in which there are more than 130 miles of trail.

Managed by both the Umatilla and Wallowa-Whitman National Forests, the preserve was originally designated as such on June 26, 1984 through enactment of Public Law 98-328, the Oregon Wilderness Act of 1984. Different from the others in that it is split up into four sections, sizes range from the smallest unit at 8,073 acres, to the largest unit at 85,412 acres. The wilderness consists of a combined total of 121,352 acres.

Situated in the northernmost section, Tower Unit is the smallest of the four units. Few trails exist here in this tree-blessed land, and those that are available provide little in the way of wide vistas.

Directly south lies the 13,911-acre Greenhorn Unit. Located in the Greenhorn Mountains, the lower slopes are heavily forested, the higher ridges open rocky areas with subalpine vegetation, subalpine fir, and whitebark pine. Lush meadows are alive with wildflowers come early summer. The largest unit, the North Fork John Day, is located between the Tower and Greenhorn units. Well over 85,000 acres strong, this portion is bisected by some 25 miles of the North Fork John Day River Canyon. Over half of the acreage consists of gentle sloping tablelands and benchlands; the remainder is comprised mostly of steep ridges and side slopes melting into the river canyon.

The North Fork John Day supports a huge population of fish with an estimated 4,500 chinook and 10,500 steelhead migrating to the North Fork John Day River spawning grounds. The system also provides good spawning and nurturing habitat for brook trout, rainbow trout, Dolly Varden, and whitefish.

Hikers may find old mining relics along the North Fork John Day River for this drainage was once a bustling gold and silver mining area in the middle to late 1800's. Look for old mining structures (there are 26 known cabins) ditches, and other hints of the thousands of folks who removed an estimated $10 million in gold and silver.

Present day miners still work along the river; in fact, about 2,000 mining claims were on file at the time of designation in 1984. Several of these claims are considered valid and these folks are currently mining their claims.

Over 13,000 acres in size, Baldy Creek is located due east of the North Fork John Day Unit in the Elkhorn Mountains. The Elkhorn Crest Trail, a National Recreation Trail, winds along the top of Elkhorn Ridge, providing see-forever views.

Solitude is often easy to find in this wilderness, but not in the fall when it is heavily used by hunters. Backpackers seeking solitude should visit in July, August, or early September. July and August tend to be the best weather months. However, rain or snow in the highest areas is not uncommon any month of the year.

Wildlife includes Rocky Mountain elk, mule deer, whitetailed deer, black bear, mountain lion, and occasionally mountain goat. Bird species include the Swainson's hawk and bald eagle.

CRAWFISH LAKE (hike 59)

Trail length: About 0.5 mile one-way.
Description: A day hike in the North Fork John Day Wilderness.
Difficulty: Moderate to strenuous.
Highlights: Scenic lake; great fishing.
Elevations: 6,600 to 6,980 feet.
Maps: North Fork John Day Wilderness Map.
Hiking season: Mid-June through November.
Permits: Trail Park Permit.
Contact: Baker Ranger District, Rt. 1, Box 1, Baker City, OR 97814; (541) 523-4476.
Directions: Reach the Crawfish Lake Trailhead by driving 10.5 miles east on Forest Road 73 from the junction of Forest Roads 73 and 52. Turn right on Forest Road 218 and drive 0.8 mile to the trailhead.
Trail info: Hike Crawfish Lake Trail 1606 by crossing a log bridge, and again crossing a stream one hundred yards or so ahead. Climb through the trees then level off and reach Crawfish Lake at 0.5 mile.

The trail continues around the west side of the lake, eventually leading to Forest Road 320. At the south end of the lake there are nice views of Hoffer Butte and Gunsight Mountain.

ELKHORN CREST (hike 60)

Trail length: About 8.7 miles one-way.
Description: A backpack trip in the North Fork John Day Wilderness.
Difficulty: Moderate.
Highlights: Spectacular views; wildlife.
Elevations: 7,131 to 8,100 feet.
Maps: North Fork John Day Wilderness Map.
Hiking season: Late June through November.
Permits: Trail Park Permit.

Contact: Baker Ranger District, Rt. 1, Box 1, Baker City, OR 97814; (541) 523-4476.
Directions: The Elkhorn Crest Trailhead is located off Forest Road 73 near the Anthony Lakes Campground, about 24 miles east of Haines. The trailhead is located just before the Anthony Lakes Campground turnoff. A sign points the way.
Trail info: Hike Elkhorn Crest Trail 1611 to the south, passing above the east shore of Black Lake after 1.0 mile. Farther on, you'll hike past stunted, twisted pines embedded in granite. Reach a crest at 2.9 miles. There's a grand view from here; Angell Peak is to the northwest; to the north see the valley below and Van Patten Butte; west/southwest point to the wilderness and beyond.

Reach the junction for Dutch Flat Saddle at 3.5 miles. Walk on over to the edge for a good view of Dutch Flat Lake. Dutch Flat Creek Trail 1607 leads to the lake in 1.0 mile. Continue across the slope via the Elkhorn Trail and reach Cunningham Saddle at 4.2 miles. Keep straight, heading across the slope to Nip and Tuck Pass at 5.4 miles. Reach the junction for Lost Lake Trail 1621 at 5.5 miles. Proceed to Lost Lake Saddle at 6.2 miles for a good view of Lost Lake to the east. Reach the wilderness boundary at 8.6 miles and a junction at 8.7 miles.

This trail description ends here, but those who would like to explore farther can hike Peavy Trail 1640 to Peavy Cabin, an old road to Cracker Creek and the old townsite of Bourne, or continue on the Elkhorn Crest Trail.

GLADE CREEK/COLD SPRING LOOP (hike 61)

Trail length: About 9.1 miles for the complete loop.
Description: A day hike or a backpack trip in the North Fork John Day Wilderness.
Difficulty: Moderate.
Highlights: Wildflowers; wildlife.
Elevations: 5,200 to 6,560 feet.

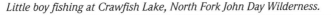

Little boy fishing at Crawfish Lake, North Fork John Day Wilderness.

Rocky mountain elk (cow).

Maps: North Fork John Day Wilderness Map.
Hiking season: Mid-June through November.
Permits: None required.
Contact: Umatilla National Forest, 2517 S.W. Hailey, Pendleton, OR 97801; (541) 276-3811.
Directions: Drive Forest Road 10 east from Dale for 11.6 miles. At this point the road forks; turn left on Forest Road 1010 and drive 8.0 miles farther to the trailhead.
Trail info: Glade Creek Trail 3014 begins off the old road near a corral. Although the trail might be difficult to find in some sections, rock cairns and blazed trees show the way.

At 1.8 miles cross a creek and reach the junction of Cold Springs Trail at 2.1 miles. Glade Creek Trail 3014 continues to the left and on to the North Fork John Day River. Hike right onto Cold Springs Trail 3008. Reach a meadow at 3.1 miles.

Upon reaching 4.9 miles and a junction with an old road, keep to the road, now hiking the road which serves as a trail. Proceed to two more junctions—one at 7.4 miles, one at 7.7 miles—before reaching the Cold Springs Trailhead at 9.0 miles. Head right on Forest Road 1010 and reach the parking area at 9.1 miles.

NORTH FORK JOHN DAY RIVER (hike 62)

Trail length: About 13.7 miles one-way.
Description: A backpack trip in the North Fork John Day Wilderness.
Difficulty: Moderate.
Highlights: Wildlife; great fishing; solitude except during hunting season.
Elevations: 5,200 to 3,936 feet.
Maps: North Fork John Day Wilderness Map.
Hiking season: Mid-June through November.
Permits: Trail Park Permit.
Contact: North Fork John Day Ranger District, P.O. Box 158, Ukiah, OR 97880; (541) 427-3231.
Directions: The trailhead begins 8.5 miles north of the small town of Granite, at a campground near the junction of Forest Road 52 and Forest Road 73.
Trail info: The North Fork John Day River Trail, a National Recreation Trail, extends for miles along the beautiful North Fork John Day River. This text describes the route to the confluence of Granite Creek. Hike North Fork Trail 3022, hiking parallel to the river. Look for miners' cabins along the way; some of them are open to the public. However, the owners ask that you leave things as they were when

you arrived.

As you hike the trail you'll see a number of jars nailed to trees, usually at about eye level. Inside each jar you'll find a photocopy of a mining claim. In the mid-to late-1800s, this region bustled with miners searching for gold and silver; miners left with roughly $10 million in gold and silver.

At about 5 miles pass the Thornburg Placer Mine, a potpourri of mining activity at one time. Soon after passing a sign "Whisker Peak" at 10.6 miles, you'll see a cabin on the left. Hike the spur trail past the cabin, then ford the river, continuing on the opposite side to a sign "Bear Gulch" in another 0.2 mile.

Reach Granite Creek and some horse corrals at 13.7 miles.

OLIVE LAKE/SADDLE RIDGE LOOP (hike 63)

Trail length: About 12.2 miles for the complete loop.
Description: A day hike or a backpack trip in the North Fork John Day Wilderness.
Difficulty: Moderate; some steep areas.
Highlights: Nice views; wildflowers; good fishing.
Elevations: 6,000 to 7,400 feet.
Maps: North Fork John Day Wilderness Map.
Hiking season: Mid-June through November.
Permits: None required.
Contact: Umatilla National Forest, 2517 S.W. Hailey, Pendleton, OR 97801; (541) 276-3811.
Directions: From Dale, travel 27.0 miles east on Forest Road 10 to Forest Road 480. Turn right and continue straight past the fork leading to the Olive Lake boat dock, reaching the trailhead at roads end in 1.0 mile.
Trail info: Hike Saddle Camp Trail 3035, an old road, and cross a creek at 0.7 mile. Reach Upper Olive Lake, which is mostly just a meadow now, after 0.9 mile. Continue along the west side, reaching the end of the road and a sign at 1.4 miles.

Continue on the trail, crossing several creeks en route to Saddle Camp and the junction to Blue Mountain Trail 6141 at 2.9 miles. Turn left (south) on Trail 6141. At 3.3 miles a rocky outcrop provides a nice view of Upper Olive Lake. Proceed to 4.9 miles where you'll begin walking an old road again, coming to the Lost Creek Trail 3002 junction at 5.3 miles.

Follow Trail 3002, which is really an old road, to the northwest. At 6.0 miles the trail forks; turn left and proceed to a junction and sign "Lost Meadow-2 miles, Desolation Rd.-4 miles" at 7.4 miles. Turn left and soon the road turns into a trail again. Reach Lost Creek at 8.6 miles and Lost Meadow at 9.4 miles. After 10.5 miles the trail meets Forest Road 10. Turn left and hike back to the turnoff to Olive Lake at 11.3 miles. Continue to the trailhead at 12.2 miles.

Mallards (hen and ducklings).

Introduction To The North Fork Umatilla Wilderness

Visitors to the North Fork Umatilla Wilderness find a rugged land where extremely steep, timbered canyons divide tree-dotted plateaus blanketed by native bunchgrass. Those visitors who enjoy fishing, will find sizeable runs of anadromous fish, and Dolly Varden trout to their liking. Also, hikers find a variety of trails to explore.

Located 30 miles east of Pendleton, Oregon, this small 20,435 acre wilderness has 27 miles of maintained trails to suit the needs of nearly everyone. Those who enjoy grand views will want to hike Ninemile Ridge. Hikers who'd rather stay below will find lush vegetation draped around the various creeks that skirt through the lower portions of the area.

The North Fork Umatilla Wilderness was designated as such by Congress on June 26, 1984 and receives protection under the Oregon Wilderness Act of 1984. Listed as wilderness for a variety of reasons, high quality water was one of the major forces behind such classification. The North Fork of the Umatilla River supports sizeable runs of anadromous fish and also provides irrigation water for downstream agriculture.

Other wilderness streams include: Buck Creek, Bear Creek, Coyote Creek, and Johnson Creek. All of the above streams contain native trout and several have spawning steelhead.

The wilderness is also known for it's excellent big game habitat (deer and elk) and is a popular hunting area each fall as hoards of hunters descend upon the region. An excellent summer range where calving, rearing, and breeding occur, the area is critical deer winter range as well.

Other mammal found here include cougar and black bear. Bird life includes blue and ruffed grouse which are common. Also, there are eagles, owls, woodpeckers (including pileated woodpeckers), and a variety of song birds.

Abundant animal life is a result of the five major community types found within the wilderness. Look for bunchgrass on shallow steep slopes, mixed conifer species, Ponderosa pine and associated species, and subalpine fir.

Wildflowers bloom in spring and early summer. Although there are no records of rare and endangered plants found here, there are several plants identified as sensitive for this region. Look for Sabin's lupine, mountain ladysslipper, (both common in the area), as well as Kruckeberg's sword fern.

Hikers—especially those hoping to capture flowers on film—should note that summers are intense in this area with highs averaging in the 80's, but often soaring to more than 100 degrees. June through September are the hottest months, with nighttime temperatures cooling down on even the hottest of days. For flower photographs, get up early or stay out late, thus avoiding the harsh rays of the mid-day sun.

Monarch butterfly.

Ox eye daisy.

NINEMILE RIDGE (hike 64)

Trail length: About 6.8 miles one-way.
Description: A long day hike or a backpack trip in the North Fork Umatilla Wilderness.
Difficulty: Moderate.
Highlights: Splendid views; wildflowers; wildlife; solitude except during hunting season.
Elevations: 2,400 to 5,100 feet.
Maps: North Fork Umatilla Wilderness Map.
Hiking season: June through November.
Permits: Trail Park Permit.
Contact: Umatilla National Forest, 2517 S.W. Hailey, Pendleton, OR 97801; (541) 276-3811.
Directions: From the junction of Oregon Highways 82 and Oregon 204 in Elgin, head west on Oregon 204, driving 3.8 miles to Forest Road 3738 (Phillips Creek Road); make a left. Travel 10.5 miles to Forest Road 31; make another left, going 3.8 miles to Ruckel Junction. Head right on Forest Road 32 for 10.2 miles to the Umatilla Campground. At the south end off the campground, turn right on Forest Road 415, driving until it ends in 0.2 mile. The trailhead is near the gate.
Trail info: Ninemile Trail 3072 begins about 100 yards or so down the road. The grade is pretty steep at times for the first part of the trail, but then it levels off a lot as you hike across Ninemile Ridge. From the ridge you'll see that much of the wilderness is very rugged, a place of forested canyons and plateaus decorated with native bunchgrass and an occasional tree.

NORTH FORK UMATILLA RIVER (hike 65)

Trail length: About 4.0 miles one-way.
Description: A long day hike or a backpack trip in the North Fork Umatilla Wilderness.
Difficulty: Easy.
Highlights: Scenic walk long the river; wildlife.
Elevations: 2,380 to 2,840 feet.
Maps: North Fork Umatilla Wilderness Map.
Hiking season: June through November.
Permits: Trail Park Permit.
Contact: Umatilla National Forest, 2517 S.W. Hailey, Pendleton, OR 97801; (541) 276-3811.
Directions: From Oregon Highway 82 at Elgin, head west on Oregon Highway 204. At 3.8 miles turn left on Forest Road 3738 (Phillips Creek Road); drive 10.5 miles to Forest Road 31. Turn left on Road 31 and reach Ruckel Junction in 3.8 miles; stay to the right, now Forest Road 32. Drive 10.2 miles to the Umatilla Campground. Upon reaching the south end of the campground, continue straight ahead 0.5 mile to the North Fork Umatilla River Trailhead.
Trail info: Hike North Fork Umatilla River Trail 6143, mostly staying in the trees. There are several creek crossings as you hike through lush vegetation.

After 4 miles the trail heads away from the river and on up to Coyote Ridge. If you opt to check it out it's a moderate grade with some steep pitches.

INTRODUCTION TO THE RED BUTTES WILDERNESS

The Red Buttes Wilderness is one of those areas that once visited, just has to be visited time and time again. Something lures a person back. It might be the steep mountain slopes, spectacular viewpoints, colorful meadows, or deep-blue lakes. Maybe it's one of the above, all of the above, or none of the above. Whatever the reason, the Red Buttes Wilderness is definitely worth exploring.

It's located near the crest of the rugged Siskiyou Mountains along the border between southwestern Oregon and northwestern California. Comprised of a chain of peaks, the Siskiyou crest forms the southern boundary; these peaks include Red Buttes, Kangaroo Mountain, and Rattlesnake Mountain.

The Siskiyou Crest serves as a watershed divide between the Rogue River to the north and the Klamath River to the south. A tributary of the popular Rogue River, the Butte Fork Applegate River begins life as its waters flow out from Azalea lake, and continue through the heart of the preserve. A small portion of the Illinois River drainage is also located here.

The wilderness consists of 20,234 acres, ranging in elevation from 3,000 feet along the Butte Fork Applegate River to 6,739 feet on top of Red Buttes. Three National Forests—the Rogue River, Siskiyou, and Klamath—manage Red Buttes which was designated wilderness by Congress in 1984. Red Buttes, the 6,739 feet high butte for which the wilderness was named, and nearby Kangaroo Mountain, are composed of weathered periodotite and serpentine. These reddish-orange mountains, along with other rock-types in the vicinity, form inhospitable but scenic terrain which supports a number of unusual plant species.

It is estimated that one quarter of Oregon's rare and endangered plants are found in the Klamath-Siskiyou Area. This is due primarily to an intermingling of climates and plant communities where northwest California and southwest Oregon meet.

Terrain is another factor in the huge assortment of plants found in the area. A dozen or so plants are believed to grow on serpentine rock which is found throughout the area. Plant growth on serpentine soil tends to be sparse, open, and stunted. In addition, some species have adapted specifically to serpentine soil and are rarely found elsewhere.

Steep slopes, some of them rocky and open, others deeply forested with pine, also form the rugged terrain. The lower slopes are forested with white fir, Shasta red fir, and Douglas-fir, with upper slope forest in the higher elevations.

There are some relatively uncommon species of trees to observe here. Two weeping evergreens, the Port Orford cedar, and the rare Brewer spruce, are found only in the Klamath-Siskiyou Mountain area. Once widespread, today researchers believe these species are bound to serpentine soils by their inability to compete with other trees where conditions are better.

Glaciation has created many interesting geologic features, including several nice lakes in the area. The lakes found at the highest regions are carved out basins formed by small glaciers.

Meadows are particularly colorful in the spring and summer months. Look for brilliant red crimson columbines, their spurred petals similar to an eagle's claw according to some folks. Also, find orange-colored tiger lilies, Washington lilies, and giant red paintbrush, too.

In addition to the many species of plant life, hikers will find an abundance of animal life. Although often hard to observe there are deer, elk, bear, and porcupine, to name just a few of the mammals found in the area. Also, there are many species of birds including gray jays and Clark's nutcrackers.

LONESOME LAKE (hike 66)

Trail length: About 9.0 miles one-way.
Description: A backpack trip in the Red Buttes Wilderness.

Backpacker in the Red Buttes Wilderness.

Oregon iris.

Difficulty: Moderate.
Highlights: Nice views; lush meadows; wonderful wildflowers; wildlife.
Elevations: 4,300 to 6,000 feet.
Maps: Red Buttes Wilderness map.
Hiking season: July through October.
Permits: Trail Park Permit.
Contact: Applegate Ranger District, 6941 Upper Applegate Rd., Jacksonville, OR 97530; (541) 899-1812.
Directions: Reach the Steve Fork Trailhead by driving from the town of Applegate. At the junction of Oregon Highway 238 and Forest Road 10, head south on Road 10 for 15 miles. Make a right on Forest Road 1030 and continue another 11 miles until the road ends at the Steve Fork Trailhead.
Trail info: Begin hiking an old road/trail and reach a fork at 0.8 mile. Trail 906 heads to the right and up to Sucker Creek Gap. (See TANNEN LAKES for details.) Stay left at the fork and reach Steve Fork Creek soon after; cross and come to the junction of Trails 905 and 906 at 1.0 mile. Turn right and reach another fork at 1.4 mile. Turn left, reaching a ridgetop at 2.9 miles.

Proceed to the Azalea Lake/Fir Glade Trail junction at 3.2 miles. Turn right onto Fir Glade Trail 955 and reach Phantom Meadows junction at 3.5 miles. The 260-foot drop in elevation and 0.8 mile hike down the unmaintained trail is well worth the effort, especially when the wildflowers are in bloom.

Continue on, reaching Azalea Lake, named for the countless western azalea plants found around it, at 6.7 miles. Washington lilies, also known as Cascade lilies, are visible as well.

Reach Lonesome Lake by hiking Butte Fork Trail 957 to the east. The trail follows the Butte Fork Applegate River which begins at Azalea Lake, and winds through lush forests to Cedar Basin.

In the middle of Cedar Basin, at 7.6 miles, reach the junction of Butte Fork Trail 957 and Fort Goff Trail 956; turn right on Fort Goff.

At 8.6 miles cross a small creek which flows from Lonesome Lake and take the trail to the right; reach the junction of an unmarked trail to Lonesome Lake at 8.8 miles.

TANNEN LAKES (hike 67)

Trail length: About 8.8 miles one-way.
Description: A backpack trip in the Red Buttes Wilderness.
Difficulty: Moderate.
Highlights: Nice views; lush meadows; wonderful wildflowers; wildlife.
Elevations: 4,300 to 5,440 feet.
Maps: Red Buttes Wilderness map.
Hiking season: July through October.
Permits: Trail Park Permit.
Contact: Illinois Valley Ranger District, 26468 Redwood Hwy., Cave Junction, OR 97523; (541) 592-2166.
Directions: Drive to Applegate, located off Oregon 238, and head south on Forest Road 10 for 15 miles. Turn right on Forest Road 1030 and continue another 11 miles until the road ends at the Steve Fork Trailhead.
Trail info: Hike the road/trail to a fork at 0.8 mile; it's not the easiest to see. Make a right onto Sucker Creek Gap Trail 906. (The trail to the left leads to LONESOME LAKE. See it for details.)

The trail passes through a rich forest, then crosses Sucker Creek at 2.4 miles. Reach Boundary Trail 1207 at 2.8 miles; a broken sign marks the junction.

Boundary Trail heads northeast and two trails go west. The one on the right leads to Sucker Creek Shelter, which is nearby and nice to visit; the one on the left, Boundary Trail 1207, leads to Tannen Lakes.

Proceed on Trail 1207 and reach another junction at 3.3 miles; Sucker Creek Trail 1237 heads north. Continue straight ahead to reach Tannen Lake. You'll reach the junction of Fehley Gulch at 5.9 miles; take the right fork, Tannen Lake Trail 1243. Reach East Tannen Lake at 7.8 miles. The second of the Tannen Lakes is at 8.8 miles.

TOWHEAD LAKE (hike 68)

Trail length: About 4.5 miles one-way.
Description: A long day hike or a backpack trip in the Red Buttes Wilderness.
Difficulty: Moderate.
Highlights: Great views; scenic lakes.
Elevations: 4,700 to 5,840 feet.
Maps: Red Buttes Wilderness map.
Hiking season: July through October.
Permits: Trail Park Permit.
Contact: Oak Knoll Ranger District, 22541 Highway 96, Klamath River, CA 96050; (916) 465-2241.
Directions: From Ruch, located off Oregon Highway 238, 8 miles east of Applegate, head south on Upper Applegate Road towards Applegate

Shelter at Sucker Creek Gap, Red Buttes Wilderness.

Rock creek, Rock Creek Wilderness.

INTRODUCTION TO THE ROCK CREEK WILDERNESS

Rock Creek is one of Oregon's least visited wilderness areas and for good reason. There are no trails. Nor will there ever be.

The 7,472 acre preserve stretches from sea level at the mighty Pacific to 2,200 feet atop a ridge near the center of the wilderness. The Siuslaw National Forest manages the area and prohibits horse travel due to fragile terrain.

The preserve was designated wilderness in 1984 with the signing of the Oregon Wilderness Act. Surrounded by roads, the Rock Creek area was never harvested, nor were roads built through it. Fortunately the land consists of some low value hardwoods and immature conifer stands.

If you could hike into the region, beginning at the ocean, you'd walk under Sitka spruce and western hemlock for the first two miles. From this point, you'd see the forest gradually shift to old-growth Douglas-fir and hemlock. Dense undergrowth nearly smothers the forest floor. Plant species include salal, sword fern and salmonberry. Rhododendrons bloom in May. Alder, bigleaf maple, and vine maple line the creeks. Wildflowers flourish in the springl look for candyflowers, monkeyflowers, asters, and foxglove to name a few.

The preserve rests 15 miles north of Florence and as with the other coast areas, receives a substantial amount of rain; sixty to eighty inches each year. Fogs blankets the coast and valleys most of the summer. Winters are usually free of snow. Spring and fall are perhaps the best times for clear sunny days.

Hardy pioneers are known to have tried homesteading within the boundaries of what is now known as the Rock Creek Wilderness. Three homesteads once existed: two on upper Big Creek and the third on lower Rock Creek. The lower Rock Creek homestead sat a short distance above the present-day Rock Creek Forest Camp. Homesteaders lived there until the mid-1940's.

Two primary creeks—Rock Creek and Big Creek—flow through the area, both draining directly into the Pacific, both supporting runs of anadromous fish.

Dam. After 20.5 miles reach the southwest end of Applegate Lake and turn left on Forest Road 1050. Continue one mile on Forest Road 1050 then turn right on Forest Road 1055. At this point you'll see a sign "Cook N Green Pass, 10 miles ahead." Follow it until you reach the junction of the Cook and Green Pass and the Pacific Crest Trail (PCT).

Trail info: From the Cook and Green Pass and PCT junction, hike the PCT to the west. At 2.3 miles come to a fork at Camp Trail 958; the PCT crosses a mining road at 2.7 miles. Reach the Lily Pad Lake junction at 3.7 miles. Head straight towards Kangaroo Springs and Towhead Lake. If you like great views take the trail to Rattlesnake Mountain; you'll see Mt. Shasta to the southeast and Mt. McLoughlin to the northeast. No doubt you'll feel as close to being on top of the world as you can for mountains of this size.

Reach Towhead by turning right at 3.7 miles and traveling a mining road. Come to a fork at 4.l miles; bear to the right and follow it past an old building to the end of the road. An old trail leads north west to Towhead lake. Bushwhack for the next 0.4 mile as you descend to Towhead Lake at 4.5 miles.

ROCK CREEK (hike 69)

Trail length: About 0.5 mile one-way.
Description: A day hike in the Rock Creek Wilderness.
Difficulty: Easy.
Highlights: Solitude; old-growth forest.
Elevations: 160 to 180 feet.
Maps: Heceta Head USGS quad.
Hiking season: Year-round.
Permits: None required.
Contact: Waldport Ranger District, P.O. Box 400, Waldport, OR 97394; (541) 563-3211.
Directions: To reach the trailhead at Rock Creek Campground, travel U.S. Highway 101, 10.6 miles south from Yachats. Turn east at the sign pointing the way to the "Rock Creek Campground" via Forest Road 514.

The campground is open during the summer so if the gate is closed you'll have to hike to the beginning of the trail. Actually, Rock Creek Trail is an old game trail and will never be maintained in this technically trailless wilderness.

Trail info: From the gate it's a nice half mile walk along the creek and through the campground to site number 16, where the unmaintained trail begins.

In another 0.5 mile the trail leads to a pretty meadow. You'll have to ford the creek to see it; the water is usually a chilly 56 degrees. In the spring you'll find a variety of flowers, including buttercups, crimson columbine, and huge skunk cabbage.

While viewing the creek, look for the American Dipper, a robin-size brown bird that walks underwater while looking for its prey.

Wood duck (drake).

INTRODUCTION TO THE ROGUE-UMPQUA DIVIDE WILDERNESS

Flowers sway in lush meadows, pine trees reach skyward in thick forests, and fish jump in the crystal clear waters of the many lakes found in the area. Amazingly, this is but a small portion of what each hiker can see and experience in the Rogue-Umpqua Divide Wilderness.

Located in southwestern Oregon, ten miles northwest of Crater Lake National Park, the Rogue-Umpqua Divide Wilderness rests on the western side of the Cascade Range. As part of the old western Cascade range of mountains, this area developed millions of years ago before the present-day Cascade Mountains were formed. As a result, ancient lake beds can be found near Mosquito Lake country in the northeast portion of the wilderness, and unique rock formations are located throughout many sections of the preserve.

Vine maple, Rogue-Umpqua Divide Wilderness.

Designated the Rogue-Umpqua Divide Wilderness in 1984 when Congress signed the Oregon Wilderness Bill into effect, the wilderness was first established as the Rogue-Umpqua Divide Roadless area in 1972. At that time approximately 50,000 acres were set aside for protection. When the 1984 Oregon Wilderness bill was signed only 33,200 acres of those original acres were designated as wilderness. However, the remaining 16,800 acres of roadless area will remain unroaded and untouched.

The sanctuary is managed by both the Umpqua and Rogue River National Forests; the Umpqua is responsible for 26,350 acres, and the Rogue manages 6,850 acres.

From a low of 2,800 feet in the Fish Lake Basin, the wilderness reaches to a high of 6,783 feet atop Rattlesnake Mountain. In between hikers will find timbered valleys and sub-alpine meadows to hike in, and lakes to swim and fish in. In addition, some of the trails follow ridgetops where spectacular views of the surrounding mountains and valleys are possible.

There are ten trailheads leading to an extensive trail system. Winding past rock formations such as Elephant Head and the Palisades, the trails provide a variety of scenery for each backpacker to enjoy. Paths lead past flowery meadows where spring visitors can delight in touching, smelling, and photographing a wide variety of brightly colored flowers, some no bigger than a coin, others, like the Washington lily, many times that size.

An assortment of wildlife might also be viewed. Mammals include elk, deer, mountain lion, black bear, bobcat, and lynx. Bird consist of bald eagles, golden eagles, and peregrine falcons, to name a few.

Mosquitoes are a pesky form of animal life found in the upper snow fields and around Fish Lake at certain times of the year. For the most part, however, the wilderness is mosquito-free, especially when hiking in the area after the month of June has passed, though carrying bug repellent is recommended anytime.

For a bug-free adventure try visiting the Rogue-Umpqua Divide in the winter months when heavy snow blankets the ground. Nordic skiers delight in the peace and quiet the secluded preserve provides. Please note, the Forest Service does not plow the roads leading to the wilderness.

Fish Lake, Rogue-Umpqua Divide Wilderness.

ABBOTT BUTTE/ELEPHANT HEAD (hike 70)

Trail length: About 4.4 miles one-way.

Description: A day hike in the Rogue-Umpqua Divide Wilderness.

Difficulty: Moderate.

Highlights: Nice views; unique rock formations.

Elevations: 5,000 to 6,131 feet.

Maps: Rogue-Umpqua Divide Wilderness map.

Hiking season: Late June through October.

Permits: None required.

Contact: Prospect Ranger District, Prospect, OR 97536; (541) 560-3623.

Directions: Reach the Abbott Butte Trailhead by driving Oregon Highway 62 to Forest Road 68, four miles south of Union Creek. Turn west on Forest Road 68; after 12.5 miles reach the Rogue-Umpqua Divide at 5,340 feet. Now turn right onto Forest Road 30 and continue 0.5 mile to Forest Road 950. The trailhead begins in 0.2 mile, at the end of Road 950.

Trail info: Rogue-Umpqua Divide Trail 1470 begins at the sign "Fish Creek Valley - 22 miles." The trail (which is sometimes an old road) leads to Windy Gap at 0.7 mile. Here, there's a nice view of Crater Lake and Mt. McLoughlin.

Pass the Cougar Butte Trail junction at 1.5 miles, continuing to the Abbott Butte junction at 2.0 miles.

Abbott Butte is a moderate 0.5-mile climb to an old fire tower where you'll get a nice view of the surrounding peaks and valleys.

Back at the junction and now at 3.0 miles, proceed to Elephant Head, passing a sign to North/South Trail 1433 at 3.4 miles. Continue on to 4.4 miles where you'll reach a couple of beaver-made ponds, and a great view of Elephant Head.

HERSHBERGER MOUNTAIN/FISH LAKE LOOP
(hike 71)

Trail length: About 13.7 miles for the complete loop.

Description: A long day hike or a backpack trip in the Rogue-Umpqua Divide Wilderness.

Difficulty: Moderate.

Highlights: Great view; wildlife.

Elevations: 3,400 to 6,000 feet.

Maps: Rogue-Umpqua Divide Wilderness map.

Hiking season: Late June through October.

Permits: None required.

Contact: Prospect Ranger District, Prospect, OR 97536; (541) 560-3623 or Tiller Ranger District, 27812 Tiller Trail Hwy., Tiller, OR 97484; (541) 825-3201.

Directions: From Union Creek, drive Oregon Highway 230 north two miles to Forest Road 6510; turn west (left) on Road 6510 and continue for 1.6 miles. Proceed on Forest Road 6520 for 0.4 mile; turn left on Forest Road 6515, driving 6.8 miles to Forest Road 530. Take Road 530, 1.6 miles to the Hershberger Mountain Trailhead.

Trail info: Hike the Rogue-Umpqua Divide Trail 1470 for 1 mile to Fish Lake Trail 1570. Turn left on Trail 1570, (the other trail will be your return), passing through Highrock Meadow then descending along side Highrock Creek. Reach Fish Lake at approximately 4 miles. Here, anglers vie for rainbow, brook, and German brown trout.

Proceed past Fish Lake, reaching Beaver Swamp Trail 1569 at just over 5 miles. Turn right and head up the trail to the Beaver Swamp Trailhead at 6.2 miles. There's a sign pointing the way to your destination, Rocky Rim Trail 1572 where you'll find outstanding views along much of the trail. Near the 10-mile mark, you'll cross a saddle—about five feet wide—with magnificent views of Diamond Peak, Mt. Bailey, and Mt. Thielsen.

Cross a couple of meadows as you continue to the Rogue-Umpqua Divide Trail 1470 at 12.4 miles; go right, hiking Trail 1470 to the trailhead.

INTRODUCTION TO THE SALMON-HUCKLEBERRY WILDERNESS

Musical waterfalls dance in thick forested river canyons, quiet pools of water reflect bank-hugging wildflowers. And from atop an array of summits and high ridges there are fabulous views of the Salmon-Huckleberry Wilderness and surrounding areas.

Steep slopes, pinnacles, cliffs, and volcanic plugs exist in a land where the elevation ranges from a low of 1,400 feet along the bountiful Salmon River, to 4,877 feet atop Salmon Butte. The Mt. Hood National Forest manages the 44,600-acre preserve, located 55 miles southeast of Portland and 15 miles southeast of Sandy.

Two major drainages—Eagle Creek and the Salmon River—penetrate the region: Both are good for fishing with major runs of steelhead, Chinook, and coho salmon returning annually to the Salmon River. Two tiny lakes—Salmon Lake and Plaza Lake—pinpoint the wilderness: Only one, Plaza Lake, appears on the map.

More than 70 miles of trails crisscross the area with the Salmon River National Recreation Trail being the most popular trail of all. A major attraction, the Salmon River Gorge displays its many waterfalls to those hiking off the main trail in the southeast portion of the preserve. Please note: Maintained trails do not lead down the steep slopes to the falls.

Western hemlock and Douglas-fir envelope the lower and mid-range slopes and canyon bottoms of the preserve, with an occasional western red cedar or red alder scattered about. In the fall, scarlet vine maple add a dash of brilliance to the scene. Those interested in rarities should look for

View from Coffman Camp, Salmon-Huckleberry Wilderness.

uncommon Alaska cedar trees on the periphery of Salmon River Meadows. Pacific Silver fir cover the upper slopes of the region.

Black bear, Roosevelt elk, and blacktail deer find refuge in the dense forest. Both elk and deer winter in the rugged lower canyon during the winter. Other animal life exists here as well, but is not so easily seen. Quiet hikers may observe cougar, fisher, and marten. Bird life includes the water ouzel, also known as a dipper. They live along creeks and rivers, walking on the river bottom, looking for larvae, bugs, and other goodies.

In June, hikers won't want to miss what should be named the "Enchanting World of Wilderness Wildflowers" show. Hike across open ridgetops, formed 10 million years before the birth of the High Cascades, all while seeing a vast array of wildflowers. While hiking across what is no more than mere foothills to the loftier peaks to the east, look for flamboyant Washington lilies and the delicate white plumes of beargrass. An abundance of pinkish rhododendrons usually blooms in June as well.

If huckleberries are your thing, look for them in late August. Watch for black bears as you forage for the luscious blue fruit on Indian Ridge, Huckleberry Mountain, Old Baldy, and Devils Peak.

Ridgetops and summits provide panoramic views of much of Oregon. In this preserve, there are no fewer than five trail-lined ridges, all worth the long climb required to get there. In addition, there are trails leading to a birds-eye view from both Salmon Butte and Wildcat Mountain.

Boulder Ridge Trail is particularly rewarding: It travels in a north-south direction, offering dramatic 360-degree views of this portion of the Beaver State. Working in cooperation with the Bureau of Land Management (BLM), the trail begins at the BLM's Wildwood Recreation Site, two miles west of Zigzag.

Although most hikers visit the area in the summer, the trails below 2,000 feet are usually snowfree in winter. Ridges are often inaccessible from November through May, sometimes until June. You can expect dry summers with 80 inches of precipitation each year.

HUCKLEBERRY MOUNTAIN (hike72)

Trail length: About 5.5 miles one-way.
Description: A long day hike in the Salmon-Huckleberry Wilderness.
Difficulty: Moderate to strenuous.
Highlights: Spectacular views; wildflowers.
Elevations: 1,200 to 4,300 feet.
Maps: Salmon-Huckleberry Wilderness map.
Hiking season: May through October.
Permits: None required.
Contact: Zigzag Ranger District, 70220 E. Highway 26, Zigzag, OR 97049; (503) 622-3191.
Directions: The trail begins at the Bureau of Land Management Wildwood Recreation Area, located off U.S. Highway 26, 3 miles west of Zigzag and 15 miles east of Sandy.
Trail info: Hike Boulder Trail 783A, crossing the Salmon River in 0.1 mile. Enter the wilderness at 1.9 miles.

The Boulder Trail becomes the Plaza Trail 783 at 4.2 miles. The trail continues to the southern boundary of the wilderness at 13 miles, but you'll reach the high point of the trail at about 5.5 miles.

PLAZA LAKE (hike 73

Trail length: About 0.8 mile one-way.
Description: A day hike in the Salmon-Huckleberry Wilderness.
Difficulty: Moderate.
Highlights: Solitude; fishing.
Elevations: 4,200 to 3,700 feet.
Maps: Salmon-Huckleberry Wilderness map.
Hiking season: May through October.
Permits: None required.
Contact: Zigzag Ranger District, 70220 E. Highway 26, Zigzag, OR 97049; (503) 622-3191.
Directions: Drive southwest from Sandy, via Oregon Highway 211; reach the junction to Oregon Highways 221 and 224 in 6.2 miles. Turn left on Oregon Highway 224, driving another 5.2 miles to Estacada where you'll make another left, staying on Highway 224. At

Plaza Lake, Salmon-Huckleberry Wilderness.

6.4 miles turn left on Forest Road 4610. A sign points the way to "Twin Springs-17 miles." Stay on Road 4610, reaching the Plaza Trail Trailhead at 18.2 miles.
Trail info: Descend 0.8 mile Plaza Lake. There isn't a sign pointing the way, but the trail is easy to find. If you miss the marker, you'll begin climbing up a road which is not unmaintained.

As you descend look for Mt. Hood in the near distance before disappearing in a lush forest of thick trees, including some immense Douglas-fir, huckleberries, and rhododendrons.

SALMON BUTTE (hike 74)

Trail length: About 4.4 miles one-way.
Description: A day hike in the Salmon-Huckleberry Wilderness.
Difficulty: Moderate to strenuous.
Highlights: Excellent views.
Elevations: 2,300 to 4,877 feet.
Maps: Salmon-Huckleberry Wilderness map.
Hiking season: May through October.
Permits: None required.
Contact: Zigzag Ranger District, 70220 E. Highway 26, Zigzag, OR 97049; (503) 622-3191.
Directions: From Zigzag, located off U.S. Highway 26, head south on Salmon River Road which eventually turns into Forest Road 2618. Pass the Green Canyons Campground at 4.6; continue another 0.3 mile and cross a bridge over the river. Follow this up the mountain 1.9 miles to a pull-out area across from Forest Road 032. If you miss the parking area, you'll reach the end of the road in 0.2 mile.

Travel up the road a little more than 200 yards to a wide open area that some have used for a camp. As the road curves to the right, see the trailhead for Trail 791 taking off to the left.
Trail info: Hike Trail 791 around the east side of the mountain; at 3.2 miles there's a grand view of Mt. Hood. At 4.1 miles reach an old abandoned road; turn right and travel another 0.3 mile to the top of Salmon Butte.

SALMON RIVER (hike 75)

Trail length: About 12.0 miles one-way.
Description: A backpack trip in the Salmon-Huckleberry Wilderness.
Difficulty: Moderate.
Highlights: Scenic streams; waterfalls (off the main trail).
Elevations: 1,600 to 2,900 feet.
Maps: Salmon-Huckleberry Wilderness map.
Hiking season: Early spring through late fall.
Permits: None required.
Contact: Zigzag Ranger District, 70220 E. Highway 26, Zigzag, OR 97049; (503) 622-3191.
Directions: Drive to Zigzag, located off U.S. Highway 26, 17 miles east

of Sandy, and head south from town on Salmon River Road (later called Forest Road 2618) for 4.9 miles. Here, you'll see a bridge over the Salmon River; park on the north side of the river at the marked trailhead.

Trail info: The Salmon River National Recreation Trail is the most popular of the trails that crisscross the area, however, you can still experience solitude if you travel several miles downriver.

Hike Salmon River Trail 742; the trail is heavily-used for the first few miles. Along the way notice the spur trails which lead down to the river. Some trails lead to waterfalls while others do not. Please use caution as the trails descend steep slopes. Hikers have died trying to view some of the waterfalls.

Pass Goat Creek at 4.8 miles and reach the end of the wilderness near the 12-mile mark. Please note, the trail does continue out of the wilderness to the trailhead at Mud Creek Road 2656-309, 1.8 miles farther.

WILDCAT MOUNTAIN (hike 76)

Trail length: About 1.8 miles one-way.
Description: A day hike in the Salmon-Huckleberry Wilderness.
Difficulty: Moderate.
Highlights: Grand views.
Elevations: 3,520 to 4,481 feet.
Maps: Salmon-Huckleberry Wilderness map.
Hiking season: May through October.
Permits: None required.
Contact: Zigzag Ranger District, 70220 E. Highway 26, Zigzag, OR 97049; (503) 622-3191.
Directions: From Sandy, drive two miles southeast via U.S. Highway 26. Turn south on paved S.E. Firwood, following the sign to "Wildcat Mountain." At 1.7 miles reach a junction; two roads take off to the left. Take the first, S.E. Wildcat Mountain Road, and continue another 10.9 miles to Forest Road 105. Turn right, coming to a fork in 0.1 mile; head left. Reach another fork 0.7 mile down the road and turn right on Forest Road 150, the right fork. Reach an old quarry and the unsigned trailhead in 0.2 mile.
Trail info: From the highest point in the quarry, look for a trail heading up the east side of a slope. Douglas Trail 781 begins to the left of two faded signs reading "Temporary Sign."

Reach a junction at 0.9 mile. Trail 782 heads to the left: stay to the right on Trail 781. At 1.2 miles you'll come to another junction to Trail 782: this one is signed "McIntyre Ridge Trail 782." (The Forest Service doesn't know why two trails are signed 782. One piece of literature claims the first Trail 782 is actually Old Douglas Camp Trail 781.) Nevertheless, stay straight on Trail 781 and there should be no problem finding Wildcat Mountain.

At 1.3 miles come to a fork where you'll see the trail has been rerouted; reach the top of the mountain at 1.8 miles.

Facing page: Mt. McLoughlin and Lake of the Woods.
Below: Aster in a meadow in Sky Lakes Wilderness.

INTRODUCTION TO THE SKY LAKES WILDERNESS

The sky reflects its deep blue image into more than two hundred pockets of water at the Sky Lakes Wilderness in southern Oregon. Centuries ago ice fields and glaciers covered this lake-blessed land. Today, hikers won't find ice fields or glaciers, but they will find remnants of the past to explore. There are volcano cores to climb and numerous lakes to fish and swim in.

The Sky Lakes Wilderness embraces both the east and west sides of the southern Oregon Cascades. Approximately six miles wide and twenty-seven miles long, the area extends from Crater Lake National Park south to Highway 140. From a low elevation of 3,800 feet in the canyon of the Middle Fork of the Rogue River, the preserve rises to a height of 9,495 feet atop Mt. McLoughlin, the highest point in southern Oregon.

Designated an official wilderness area in 1984, Sky Lakes consists of 113,413 acres, all managed by the Rogue River and Winema National Forests.

More than 200 lakes dot the landscape, ranging in size from mere ponds to lakes of 30 or 40 acres. Many of the lakes provide a grand opportunity for those who enjoy fishing.

If huckleberries are more to your liking, you'll find many of them throughout much of the wilderness. Located on both the east and west sides of the Cascades, huckleberries can be found while hiking many of the Sky Lakes Trails, but Wickiup Trail is the best bet for lots of mouth-watering huckleberries.

In addition to an abundance of fish and berries, there are nearly two dozen tree species to observe and countless species of wildflowers bloom during the late spring and early summer months. In the lowlands, hikers see trees such as the Pacific Yew, and in the high country there are mountain hemlock and subalpine fir. Shasta red fir dominates much of the area, as does lodgepole pine, especially prevalent in the Oregon Desert. Flowers and plants consist of the columbine, kinnikinnick, and huckleberry.

Wildlife is abundant. Roosevelt elk exist in all areas, especially the northern sections. Deer live here too. On the west side of the Cascades there are black-tailed deer and on the east side hikers will find mule deer. On or near the crest of the Cascades the two species meet and interbreed. Other common mammals include porcupine, chipmunk, coyote, and black bear.

Sky Lakes Wilderness can be visited anytime of the year. During the winter months it is possible to cross-country ski over the heavy snow layer which blankets the Cascades. However, backpackers will have to wait until mid-June or mid-July to find snowfree trails. The only downside to an early summer visit are the mosquitoes, which are fierce and can make hiking miserable. The best time to visit is August or later.

Little moisture falls from June to October providing relatively dry excursions into the wilderness. Except for an occasional summer thunderstorm, there is little chance of getting rained on.

The nice weather provides many with an opportunity to climb 9,495-foot Mt. McLoughlin, located in the southern portion of the wilderness. The trail to Mt. McLoughlin's summit is not technically difficult, but should only be attempted by persons in good physical condition. The trail begins with a climb through dense forest to timberline. Above timberline there isn't an actual trail, but circles and crosses painted on boulders mark the way. From the top of the peak hikers are rewarded with a spectacular panorama; on a clear day they see south to Mt. Shasta and north to Crater Lake.

DEVILS PEAK LOOP (hike 77)

Trail length: About 25.5 miles for the complete loop.
Description: A backpack trip in the Sky Lakes Wilderness.
Difficulty: Moderate to difficult.
Highlights: Great views upon exiting the trees.
Elevations: 5,840 to 7,582 feet.
Maps: Sky Lakes Wilderness map.

Hiking season: Late June through October.

Permits: None required.

Contact: Klamath Ranger District, 1936 California Ave., Klamath Falls, OR 97601; (541) 885-3400.

Directions: From the junction of U.S. Highway 97 and Oregon Highway 140, just south of Klamath Falls, travel about 28 miles northwest via Oregon Highway 140. Upon reaching Forest Road 3651, which is approximately 5 miles east of Lake of the Woods, travel north for about 10 miles to the trailhead at Cold Springs Camp.

Trail info: Hike the Cold Springs Trail 3710, reaching a fork at 0.7 mile; take the left fork, staying on Trail 3710. The trail on the right will be your return trail.

After 2 miles reach the Sky Lakes Trail junction; go left on Sky Lakes Trail 3762, and proceed to the Pacific Crest Trail (PCT) at 3.8 miles; head north (right) on the PCT.

Reach the 7,300-foot saddle between Devils Peak and Lee Peak—the highest point on Oregon's section of the PCT— at 11.9 miles. A spur trail leads from the summit to the top of 7,582-foot Devils Peak for a wonderful 360 degree view.

For the return hike, head back down (south) on the PCT to Snow Lakes Trail 3739, where you'll make a left, coming to the first of many upcoming lakes at 14.7 miles.

At Trappers Lake you'll begin hiking the Sky Lakes Trail 3762, going south past Lake Sonya to the Isherwood Trail junction at 21 miles. Turn right on Isherwood Trail 3729, hiking past several lakes before reaching another Isherwood/Sky Lakes Trail junction at 22.5 miles. Make a left onto Sky Lakes Trail 3762, hiking to South Rock Trail in 0.5 mile. Go right (south), hiking South Rock Creek Trail 3709 to the Cold Springs Trail and then back to the trailhead.

HEAVENLY TWIN LAKES LOOP (hike 78)

Trail length: About 7.2 miles for the complete loop.

Description: A day hike or backpack trip in the Sky Lakes Wilderness.

Difficulty: Easy to moderate.

Highlights: Scenic lakes; wildlife.

Elevations: 5,840 to 6,035 feet.

Maps: Sky Lakes Wilderness map.

Hiking season: June through October.

Permits: None required.

Contact: Klamath Ranger District, 1936 California Ave., Klamath Falls, OR 97601; (541) 885-3400.

Directions: From the junction of U.S. Highway 97 and Oregon Highway 140, just south of Klamath Falls, travel about 28 miles northwest via Oregon Highway 140. Upon reaching Forest Road 3651, which is approximately 5 miles east of Lake of the Woods, travel north for about 10 miles to the trailhead at Cold Springs Camp.

Trail info: Hike Cold Springs Trail 3710 to the junction of the Cold Springs/South Rock Creek Trails at 0.7 mile. Bear to the left and continue on the Cold Springs Trail. (This loop returns via the trail to your right, the South Rock Creek Trail).

Proceed to the Cold Springs/Sky Lakes Trails junction at 2.4 miles. Turn right onto Sky Lakes Trail 3762, reaching the Isherwood Trail junction at 2.7 miles. Now the lake-filled loop begins.

Turn left on Isherwood Trail 3729 and come to two lakes—Lake Natasha and Lake Elizabeth—at 2.9 miles. Continue to the emerald blue waters of Isherwood Lake, a great swimming lake, at 3.2 miles. Also, there are a few, small unnamed lakes in this area just waiting to be explored.

Sunrise Sky Lakes Wilderness.

Samoyed at Puck Lake, Sky Lakes Wilderness.

Follow the trail around the lake, through the trees, reaching the junction of Isherwood Lake/Sky Lakes Trails at 4.2 miles; turn right on Sky Lakes Trail 3762. Here you'll find the largest of the Heavenly Twin Lakes—Big Heavenly Twin Lake.

Between Big and Little Heavenly Twin Lakes you'll come to the South Rock Creek Trail 3709 at 4.7 miles. Follow this trail back to the trailhead at 7.2 miles.

MT. MCLOUGHLIN (hike 79)

Trail length: About 5.0 miles one-way.
Description: A day hike in the Sky Lakes Wilderness.
Difficulty: Moderate to strenuous.
Highlights: Outstanding 360-degree views.
Elevations: 5,560 to 9,495 feet.
Maps: Sky Lakes Wilderness map.
Hiking season: June through October.
Permits: None required.
Contact: Klamath Ranger District, 1936 California Ave., Klamath Falls, OR 97601; (541) 885-3400 or Butte Falls Ranger District, P.O. Box 227, Butte Falls, OR 97522; (541) 865-3581.
Directions: From the junction of U.S. Highway 97 and Oregon Highway 140, just south of Klamath Falls, travel about 33 miles northwest via Oregon Highway 140. Upon reaching Forest Road 3661, which is marked with a sign pointing to the Fourmile Lake Campground, travel north for 2.9 miles to a junction. Make a left on Forest Road 3650 and drive another 0.2 mile to the trailhead.
Trail info: Hike Mt. McLoughlin Trail 3716 through the woods, soon crossing a bridge over Cascade Canal. Merge with the Pacific Crest Trail (PCT) 2000 after 1.0 mile. Keep to the right, traveling another 0.2 mile to Freye Lake junction. Continue another quarter mile or so to a point where the PCT takes off to Fourmile Lake; keep left to Mt. McLoughlin.

As you climb above treeline, the forest becomes littered with rocks and boulders. Rock cairns, blazed trees, and red/green marks on various rocks mark the trail.

The trail peters out once near the main ridge leading to the summit. Here there are vertical dropoffs, vast bowls to gaze down upon, and maybe a snowfield or two. Loose shale and gravel can make the going tough. When the easy-to-follow portion of the trail ends near an old telephone pole, follow the arrows pointing up the slope. Once up on the ridge, boulder-hop your way up the mountain, following the ridge to the summit.

Each year a number of people become disoriented or lost on the way down. Be aware of your surroundings; do not be tempted by shortcuts and false trails.

PUCK LAKES (hike 80)

Trail length: About 2.6 miles one-way.
Description: A day hike or backpack trip in the Sky Lakes Wilderness.
Difficulty: Moderate.
Highlights: Scenic lakes; wildlife.
Elevations: 6,000 to 6,450 feet.
Maps: Sky Lakes Wilderness map.
Hiking season: June through October.
Permits: None required.
Contact: Klamath Ranger District, 1936 California Ave., Klamath Falls, OR 97601; (541) 885-3400.
Directions: Reach the Nannie Creek Trailhead by traveling north on Westside Road past Rocky Point (located on the northwest shore of Upper Klamath Lake), about 31 miles northwest of Klamath Falls) to Forest Road 3484. Turn left and follow the road until it ends in about 5.5 miles.
Trail info: Nannie Creek Trail 3707 is a tree-covered trail which begins with a series of switchbacks for the first 0.8 mile as it winds up the slope then levels off. Reach South Puck Lake at 2.6 miles. As you may have guessed, North Puck Lake is located to the north of South Puck Lake.

SEVEN LAKES BASIN (hike 81)

Trail length: About 11.9 miles one-way.
Description: A backpack trip in the Sky Lakes Wilderness.
Difficulty: Moderate.
Highlights: Scenic lakes; wildlife; wildflowers.
Elevations: 5,420 to 6,600 feet.
Maps: Sky Lakes Wilderness map.
Hiking season: Late June through October.
Permits: None required.
Contact: Klamath Ranger District, 1936 California Ave., Klamath Falls, OR 97601; (541) 885-3400 or Butte Falls Ranger District, P.O. Box 227, Butte Falls, OR 97522; (541) 865-3581.
Directions: Reach the Sevenmile Trailhead by driving four miles west on Nicholson Road from the small town of Fort Klamath. Turn left on Forest Road 3300 for 0.2 mile then turn right on Forest Road 3334. Follow Road 3334 until it ends at the trailhead, 6 miles from Nicholson Road.
Trail info: Hike Sevenmile Trail 3703 to the junction of the Pacific Crest Trail (PCT) at 1.8 miles; turn left, now hiking southwest on the PCT.

Continue to the PCT/Seven Lakes Trail junction at 4.4 miles; go right on Seven Lakes Trail 981, reaching Grass Lake at 4.8 miles. Proceed to the Lake Ivern/Seven Lakes Trails at 5.3 miles. Middle

Fungus, Sky Lakes Wilderness.

Lake is located across the trail. Turn right on Lake Ivern Trail 994, hiking past North Lake to Lake Ivern at 7.2 miles.

So far you've passed four of the seven lakes located in Seven Lakes Basin. To reach the remaining three, head back to the junction of Lake Ivern/Seven Lakes Trail at 9.1 miles. Seven Lakes Trail parallels the east side of Middle Lake and reaches Cliff Lake at 9.7 miles.

Continue on to South Lake at 10.1 miles and from there proceed to the Seven Lakes/Alta Lake Trails junction at 10.9 miles; turn right on Alta Lake Trail 979 and reach Alta Lake at 11.3 miles. You'll reach the north end of this long lake at 11.9 miles.

STUART FALLS (hike 82)

Trail length: About 11.7 miles one-way.
Description: A backpack trip in the Sky Lakes Wilderness.
Difficulty: Moderate.
Highlights: Oregon Desert; wonderful falls; wildflowers.
Elevations: 5,420 to 6,680 feet.
Maps: Sky Lakes Wilderness map.
Hiking season: Late June through October.
Permits: None required.
Contact: Klamath Ranger District, 1936 California Ave., Klamath Falls, OR 97601; (541) 885-3400 or Butte Falls Ranger District, P.O. Box 227, Butte Falls, OR 97522; (541) 865-3581.
Directions: Reach the Sevenmile Trailhead by driving four miles west on Nicholson Road from the small town of Fort Klamath. Turn left on Forest Road 3300 for 0.2 mile then turn right on Forest Road 3334. Follow Road 3334 until it ends at the trailhead, 6 miles from Nicholson Road.
Trail info: Hike Sevenmile Trail 3703 to the junction of the Pacific Crest Trail (PCT) at 1.8 miles; turn right onto the PCT and head towards Crater Lake, 10.5 miles away.

After 2.0 miles see a trail leading to Ranger Springs, 1.0 mile to the west. Spring water bubbles and flows in large quantities year-round at this scenic spring. Back on the PCT, continue to 6.3 miles and the turn-off for Jack Spring. (This spring is 0.5 mile west).

Proceed through the flat Oregon Desert where sparse lodgepoles grow in twisted, bizarre shapes. At 7.9 miles reach the junction of the PCT and the Stuart Falls Trails; go northwest on Stuart Falls Trail 1078. Reach the Lucky Camp Trail junction at 10.5 miles, and the Upper Red Blanket Trail at 11.4 miles. Stuart Falls is just beyond, at 11.7 miles.

TRAPPERS LAKE (hike 83)

Trail length: About 5.0 miles one-way.
Description: A day hike or backpack trip in the Sky Lakes Wilderness.
Difficulty: Easy to strenuous.
Highlights: Scenic lake; wildlife.
Elevations: 4,627 to 5,938 feet.
Maps: Sky Lakes Wilderness map.
Hiking season: June through October.
Permits: None required.
Contact: Klamath Ranger District, 1936 California Ave., Klamath Falls, OR 97601; (541) 885-3400.
Directions: Reach the Cherry Creek Trailhead, by driving Westside Rd. north from Rocky Point (located on the northwest shore of Upper Klamath Lake) to Forest Road 3450; take Road 3450 until it ends at the trailhead in 2.0 miles.
Trail info: Hike Cherry Creek Trail 3708, following Cherry Creek for the first 1.4 miles. Mosquitoes can be horrendous in this area so be sure to bring plenty of bug repellent.

After 3.5 miles the trail climbs at a rapid rate; reach the Sky Lakes Trail/Cherry Creek Trail junction at 5.0 miles. Trappers Lake is located just across the trail. Margurette Lake is a mere 0.2 mile away. Hike Sky Lakes Trail 3762 around the north end of Trappers Lake and continue to Divide Trail 3717. Margurette Lake is on your right.

INTRODUCTION TO THE STRAWBERRY MOUNTAIN WILDERNESS

Strawberry Mountain Wilderness is a magical place with much to offer. There are breathtaking views, crystal clear mountain lakes, red-tailed hawks soaring overhead, prairie falcons diving on unsuspecting prey, wildflowers, and the pleasant beauty of Canyon Creek.

Originally established in April, 1942, as the Strawberry Mountain Wild Area, the area first consisted of 33,000 acres. With the enactment of the 1964 Wilderness Act, however, the name was changed to the Strawberry Mountain Wilderness. In 1984, the Oregon Wilderness Act came into effect and the total acreage was increased to its present day size of 68,700 acres. Located east of John Day, Oregon, the wilderness is managed solely by the Malheur National Forest.

From a low of 4,800 feet to a high of 9,038 feet atop Strawberry Mountain, the area is comprised of five of the seven major life zones found in North America, one of the few places in the Pacific Northwest where this occurs in such a small area. A visit to Strawberry will include everything from sagebrush and juniper, to ponderosa pine, lodgepole pine, and subalpine fir. In addition, there are countless species of plant life to observe, including an array of colorful wildflowers.

Strawberry Mountain dominates the area, holding honors as not only the highest point in the preserve, but the highest point in the Strawberry Mountain Range as well. A trip to the top of this mountain is well worth the effort for you will feel as though you can see forever.

At the lower regions there is lush vegetation where you may find

Creek goldenrod.

Strawberry Lake, Strawberry Mountain Wilderness.

Mountain.) Smaller mammals include porcupine, beaver, mink, and marten. Avian creatures include more than 100 species of bird life. Look for blue and ruffed grouse, as well as, peregrine and prairie falcons, various species of owls, and golden and bald eagles to name a few.

HIGH LAKE (hike 84)

Trail length: About 7.7 miles one-way.
Description: A backpack trip in the Strawberry Mountain Wilderness.
Difficulty: Moderate to strenuous.
Highlights: Nice views; side trips to various lakes; wildflowers.
Elevations: 5,773 to 8,172 feet.
Maps: Strawberry Mountain Wilderness map.
Hiking season: July through November.
Permits: None required.
Contact: Prairie City Ranger District, P.O. Box 337, Prairie City, OR 97869; (541) 820-3311.
Directions: From Prairie City, located off U.S. Highway 26, go south on Main Street, following signs to Bridge Street (County Road 60) at 0.4 mile; follow Road 60 south for 6.6 miles to a fork. Head left on Forest Road 6001; travel another 4.0 miles to the trailhead at Strawberry Campground.
Trail info: Hike Strawberry Basin Trail 375 to the junction of Slide Lake at 1.0 mile. Keep right and reach another junction to Slide Lake just before reaching Strawberry Lake. At the Slide Lake/Strawberry Basin junction head left to a fork at 1.4 miles; stay right on Slide Basin Trail 372 to a junction at 2.4 miles. Continue to the right on Trail 372 until it merges with Skyline Trail 385 at 3.4 miles.

Continue straight to the Slide Lake junction at 4.0 miles. If you'd like to see the lake, turn left and reach the lake in 0.2 mile. Hike to the south end of Slide Lake and over a small hill to Little Slide Lake.

Back on Skyline Trail 385 hike to the junction of Mud Lake Trail 379 at 5.7 miles. Stay to the right on Trail 385 to a high point at 8,172 feet. (There's a spur trail north for a fantastic 360-degree view.) Reach High Lake at 7.7 miles.

INDIAN CREEK BUTTE (hike 85)

Trail length: About 9.6 miles one-way.
Description: A backpack trip in the Strawberry Mountain Wilderness.
Difficulty: Moderate to strenuous.
Highlights: Magnificent ponderosa pines; wildlife; wildflowers; grand views; solitude except during hunting season.
Elevations: 4,800 to 7,760 feet.
Maps: Strawberry Mountain Wilderness map.
Hiking season: July through November.
Permits: None required.
Contact: Prairie City Ranger District, P.O. Box 337, Prairie City, OR 97869; (541) 820-3311.

Blue grouse (adult).

scrumptious huckleberries to munch on. Also to be found are small headwater streams, some of which support fish life. These include, the Middle and East Forks of Canyon Creek, as well as, Strawberry, Berry, Onion, Redd, and Big Creeks.

Six of the seven lakes in the area also support fish life, the most popular being Strawberry Lake. Thirty-two acres in size, Strawberry Lake is the largest lake, furnishing the largest fish as a result. Other good fishing lakes (although the fish are small) include High Lake, the two Slide Lakes, and Little Strawberry Lake.

While fishing is certainly a popular pastime for those visiting the area, there are many other recreational opportunities available. In addition to backpacking, visitors can day hike, observe and photograph wildlife and scenery, explore, swim, horseback ride, and find that rare commodity—seclusion. During the fall, the area is used by deer and elk hunters. In the winter and spring months, folks visit the area on snowshoes and cross-country skis.

Another area of interest is the Canyon Creek Research Natural Area, located in the southwest portion of the wilderness. A hike through should be a real treat for those who enjoy walking through large stands of ponderosa pine.

There are about 150 miles of maintained trail linking various points, some of which follow the footsteps of the trappers, fur traders, and miners of long ago. Gold was discovered along Canyon Creek in 1862, and soon after miners arrived to establish their claims. Today hikers can still see many of these abandoned mines along the north side of the Strawberry Range.

Perhaps one of the greatest thrills is the chance to view wildlife. If you're lucky, you may see deer, elk, bear, cougar, and California bighorn sheep. (About 20 bighorn sheep live near the west end of Canyon

Fisherman at Strawberry Lake, Strawberry Mountain Wilderness.

Directions: From the junction of U.S. Highway 395 and U.S. Highway 26 in downtown John Day, go south on U.S. Highway 395 (South Canyon Blvd.) for 9.8 miles. Go left on County Road 65, traveling 2.8 miles, then turning left again on Forest Road 6510. Continue 1.6 miles to Forest Road 812; go 2.7 miles to the East Fork Canyon Creek Trailhead.

Trail info: Hike East Canyon Creek Trail 211, seeing giant ponderosa after about 2 miles. This amazing forest is part of the Canyon Creek Research Natural Area.

Cross several creeks as you continue on, coming to a good view of Indian Creek Butte at 7.6 miles. At 8.7 miles reach a spring and junction at 8.7 miles; take Table Mountain Trail 217, climbing to Table Mountain Cutoff Trail 217A. Turn left, reaching an old sign at 9.4 miles; once you pass a large rock cairn you'll have to hike off the trail and up the southwest slope to the top of Indian Creek Butte.

Giant red paintbrush.

STRAWBERRY MOUNTAIN (hike 86)

Trail length: About 6.2 miles one-way.

Description: A long day hike or a backpack trip in the Strawberry Mountain Wilderness.

Difficulty: Moderate to strenuous.

Highlights: Spectacular views; wildflowers; wildlife.

Elevations: 5,773 to 9,038 feet.

Maps: Strawberry Mountain Wilderness map.

Hiking season: July through November.

Permits: None required.

Contact: Prairie City Ranger District, P.O. Box 337, Prairie City, OR 97869; (541) 820-3311.

Directions: From Prairie City, located off U.S. Highway 26, go south on Main Street, following signs to Bridge Street (County Road 60) at 0.4 mile; follow Road 60 south for 6.6 miles to a fork. Head left on Forest Road 6001; travel another 4.0 miles to the trailhead at Strawberry Campground.

Trail info: Hike Strawberry Basin Trail 375 to the junction of Slide Lake at 1.0 mile. Keep to the right, passing another junction to Slide Lake just before Strawberry Lake; keep to the right, reaching the north end of Strawberry Lake at 1.2 miles.

Continue through the trees around the east side of the lake, climbing to Strawberry Falls at 2.5 miles. Switchback to the top of the falls, crossing over a bridge at 2.7 miles. Continue straight ahead (there's a spur leading to Little Strawberry Lake off to the left), following the trail to 3.0 miles. Walk to the edge of the ridge for a wonderful view of Strawberry Lake and beyond.

You'll skirt some meadows as you proceed, reaching the top of a ridge at 5.1 miles. Hike the west side of the ridge reaching the junction of Onion Creek Trail 368 at 5.2 miles. Turn right onto Trail 368 and climb to another junction at 5.9 miles. Turn left on Trail 368B, reaching the top of the mountain at 6.2 miles.

INTRODUCTION TO THE TABLE ROCK WILDERNESS

Steep slopes, rock outcrops, basalt columns, dense forest, fantastic views, dainty wildflowers, precious ferns, mouth-watering huckleberries, solitude, and a rich history. That, and much more describes the Table Rock Wilderness.

Unique among all but one of Oregon's wilderness areas, the Table Rock Wilderness is managed not by the U.S. Forest Service, but by the Bureau of Land Management (BLM). (The BLM manages a portion of the Wild Rogue Wilderness as well.) At 5,750 acres, Table Rock is one of the smallest preserves in the state. Nevertheless, size has little to do with beauty or solitude—both are plentiful here.

Designated wilderness when President Ronald Reagan signed into law the Oregon Wilderness Act of 1984, Table Rock rests on the west slope of the mighty Cascade Mountains, 19 miles (by road) southeast of Molalla, and 40 air miles southeast of Portland.

The nine-square-mile preserve is a prime example of forest typical of the western foothills of the Cascade Mountains. A perpetual forest of Douglas-fir and western hemlock gives way to noble fir and cedar at higher elevations. Rhododendrons and ferns grow in masses on the lower slopes. (Unfortunately, a checker-board of severe forest practices surrounds the area. In fact, Table Rock is the last sizable hunk of undeveloped forest in the Molalla River drainage.)

From early June through mid-July, a vast array of wildflowers carpet meadows. Look for such rarities as the tiny, sparsely petaled, Gorman's aster. Others include the Oregon sullivantia, fringed pinesap, Shasta lily, Clackamas iris, Hall's isopyrum, and smooth-leaved douglasia. If fresh berries bring a smile to your face, then you'll be grinning from ear to ear; try Alaska blueberry, blue and huckleberry, and trailing blackberry.

From the 4,881-foot mark at Table Rock's summit, to a low of 1,300 feet along the west end of the wilderness, hikers pass through four distinct vegetation zones: alpine, subalpine, montane and foothill.

Immature red-tailed hawks on the nest.

A diversity of animal life exists. Bird life includes the turkey vulture, pileated woodpecker, red-tailed hawk, golden eagle, and several types of owls. The spotted owl lives here, along with both the pygmy and great horned owls. In addition, look for an abundant population of blue grouse. Mammals consist of black bear, Roosevelt elk, coyote, possibly mountain lion, black-tailed deer. Small mammals include the porcupine, pika, bobcat, mountain beaver, and snowshoe hares.

No doubt, the Northern Molalla—a small tribe of Native Americans once occupying the rugged foothills between the Willamette Valley and the High Cascades—found superb hunting and fruit-gathering grounds here. The Table Rock Historic Trail, is a remnant of an old Molalla trail. The Molalla trail led from the lowlands to present-day Bull of the Woods Wilderness, and on into the High Cascades and central Oregon.

Common garter snake eating a bullfrog.

75

Juvenile blue grouse.

INTRODUCTION TO THE THREE SISTERS WILDERNESS

Lofty mountain peaks search for the heavens in the Three Sisters Wilderness. Mighty pines stand tall, swaying in the breeze. In the summer, squirrels scamper about, chattering all the while. Clear blue liquid highways begin near age-old glaciers; only a trickle at first, but fast becoming a creek or river. More than 350 azure lakes dot the land like jewels, and flowers carpet the landscape. Backpackers flock to the area for this is Oregon's busiest wilderness area.

The Three Sisters—once named Faith, Hope, and Charity, by pioneer missionaries—and the mountains for which the wilderness was named, dominate the landscape. In the mid-1800s, weary travelers used them as pilot-peaks to steer them over the rugged inland plateau. The mountains still attract travelers, but these are outdoor enthusiasts with hiking, fishing, backpacking, mountain climbing, and photography on their minds.

Ranging from a low of 1,850 feet to a high of 10,358 feet, the preserve is located in and managed by both the Willamette and Deschutes National Forests. The wilderness first gained protection in 1937. Established as a Primitive Area, it was later reclassified as wilderness in 1957. In 1964, it became part of the Congressionally-established National Wilderness Preservation System.

There are approximately 280 miles of trail within the 34-mile long, 285,202-acre preserve, including 42 miles of the Pacific Crest Trail, known as the PCT. Trails lead through varied terrain. Most begin in dense forests of Douglas-fir on the western slopes and ponderosa pine on the eastern slopes. Hikers pass through western white pine, Engelmann spruce, white fir, western red cedar, western hemlock, mountain hemlock, lodgepole pine, alpine fir, and whitebark pine.

Flowers blanket numerous meadows. Melted snow feeds blue lupine, red Indian paintbrush, heather, arnica, larkspur, bluebells, wild sunflowers, avalanche lily, elephant head, and countless others.

Tall mountain peaks command attention in the preserve. From atop 10,358 foot South Sister, Oregon's third highest peak, hikers enjoy a summit crater filled with snow and ice most of the year. During a warm spell, the ice melts and like magic, an aqua-blue lake appears. Oregon's highest lake tempts few hikers to take an icy dip.

"Shorter" peaks are visible from South Sisters summit. See Middle Sister (10,053 feet), and North Sister (10,094 feet) to the north. On a clear day, Washington's Mt. Rainer, an amazing 180 miles distant, is visible as well.

Although named the Three Sisters, researchers believe they are by no means "sisters." Some say the label should read the "Mother and Two Daughters" for the North Sister is much older than the Middle and South Sisters.

Sixteen glaciers rest, as they have for millions of years, on the slopes of four major mountains in the Three Sisters Wilderness. Today, the glaciers have diminished considerably; at one time they covered the mountains down to their 4,000 foot bases.

Mountain climbing is popular here. The Three Sisters attract climbers and, remarkably, some ascend all three peaks in one day. Both expert mountaineers and school children climb South Sister. The north and east slopes are challenging; the southern route, however, is but one long climb. See SOUTH SISTER for more details.

Climbing mountains is challenging and dangerous. Unfortunately, accidents are a fairly common occurrence. The Forest Service warns that rescue teams are rarely able to reach an accident victim in less than 6 to 12 hours. Sometimes, rescue attempts may take more than 24 hours.

Whether climbing mountains or sauntering along the trail, you may see a variety of animal life. Columbia black-tailed deer, mule deer, Roosevelt elk, and black bear are common. Cougar inhabitat the area as well. Many small animals make their home here. These include mink, marten, raccoon, porcupine, bobcat, weasel, and coyote. Bird life includes blue and ruff grouse, and bald eagles.

Three archeological sites—evidently Molalla camps—have been identified in the area. As of May 8, 1979, all three appear on the National Register of Historic Places with the State Historic Preservation Office. There's also evidence of early Euro-Americans traveling the Molalla trail. In fact, surveyors from the General Land Office used the trail in 1882 and 1897. They mapped and recorded camps along the trail as well as the trail itself.

Steep trails plague portions of the Table Rock Wilderness, making travel difficult at times for both those on foot and riding horseback. The Table Rock Historic Trail is particularly steep in some sections, but the BLM claims, "the steepest grades (30-40%) were rerouted a few years ago and now most of the trail has grades between 10 and 25 percent."

TABLE ROCK (hike 87)

Trail length: About 2.5 miles one-way.
Description: A day hike in the Table Rock Wilderness.
Difficulty: Moderate.
Highlights: Spectacular views; wildlife; wildflowers; solitude; basalt columns.
Elevations: 3,760 to 4,881 feet.
Maps: Table Rock Wilderness map.
Hiking season: Mid-June through October.
Permits: None required.
Contact: Bureau of Land Management, 1717 Fabry Road S.E., Salem, OR 97306; (503) 375-5646.
Directions: At the east edge of Molalla, off Oregon Highway 211, you'll come to a fork; go right, traveling S. Mathias Road. The road changes to S. Freyer Park Road as you continue 2.2 miles to a junction; head right on S. Dickey Prairie Road. Proceed 5.2 miles and cross the Molalla River, where there is another name change. Now this is S. Molalla Road. Drive 12.7 miles to the junction of Middle Fork and Copper Creek Roads. Make a left on Middle Fork Road and proceed 2.6 miles to the Table Rock Access Road; turn right, traveling another 6.6 miles to the marked trailhead.
Trail info: Hike New Table Rock Trail, reaching Table Rock's north face at 1.2 miles; come to a junction at 1.8 miles. Hike to the left, reaching the top of Table Rock in 2.5 miles.

BLACK CRATER (hike 88)

Trail length: About 4.0 miles one-way.
Description: A day hike in the Three Sisters Wilderness.

South Sister, Three Sisters Wilderness.

Difficulty: Moderate to strenuous.
Highlights: Stunning views.
Elevations: 4,909 to 7,251 feet.
Maps: Three Sisters Wilderness map.
Hiking season: July through October.
Permits: Wilderness Permit; Trail Park Permit.
Contact: Bend Ranger District, 1230 NE 3rd, Bend, OR 97701; (541) 388-5664.
Directions: From Sisters, travel west on Oregon Highway 242, driving 11.8 miles the Black Crater Trailhead, located just prior to Windy Point. (Oregon Highway 242 is closed during the winter months. Check with the Forest Service for opening dates; it usually opens sometime in June or July.)
Trail info: Hike Black Crater Trail 4058 through the trees and across open slope to the summit at 4.0 miles. From the old lookout you'll see south to North and South Sister, Broken Top, and Mt. Bachelor. In addition to extensive lava fields to the north, you'll also see Mt. Washington, Three Fingered Jack, Mt. Jefferson and Mt. Hood. See the town of Sisters and the mountains and high desert beyond when looking east. Look down 700 feet to the north for a view into the actual crater.

MINK LAKE LOOP (hike 89)

Trail length: About 20.1 miles for the complete loop.
Description: A backpack trip in the Three Sisters Wilderness.
Difficulty: Moderate.
Highlights: Numerous lakes; some wildflowers.
Elevations: 5,150 to 5,760 feet.
Maps: Three Sisters Wilderness map.
Hiking season: July through October.
Permits: Wilderness Permit; Trail Park Permit.
Contact: Bend Ranger District, 1230 NE 3rd, Bend, OR 97701; (541) 388-5664 or McKenzie Ranger District, State Highway 126, McKenzie Bridge, OR 97413; (541) 822-3381.
Directions: The loop begins at the Six Lakes Trailhead, 35 miles west of Bend via the Cascades Lakes Highway (Oregon Highway 46). A sign "Six Lakes Trailhead" points the way.

Trail info: Hike Six Lakes Trail 14 to a spur trail at 0.9 mile; it leads to the northeast side of Blow Lake. Turn left toward Doris Lake, which you'll reach at 2.2 miles.

Continue to a junction at 3.2 miles; stay to the right and hike towards the Pacific Crest Trail (PCT) at 5.1 miles. The trail off to the left is the return trail for this loop. To the right, the PCT heads to Island Lake and north to Canada. Hike straight ahead to Vera Lake at 5.3 miles.

Continue past Vera Lake, and reach a junction at 7.2 miles; a sign points the way to Goose Lake located close to the junction. To proceed to Mink Lake, head left to Porky Lake, at 7.7 miles. Come to the Mud Lake junction at 8.1 miles; keep straight and reach the junction to Mink Lake at 8.3 miles. Turn right and at 8.8 miles you'll come to a fork and a view of Mink Lake, the largest of the Three Sisters Lakes. Keep right to continue the loop around the lake and reach the Mink Lake Shelter at 8.9 miles.

At 9.9 miles find the Junction Lake junction; stay straight and reach the Elk Creek Trailhead junction at 10.0 miles. Again keep straight, now hiking towards South Lake. Reach the PCT junction at 11.7 miles.

Turn left and continue to Mac Lake at 12.1 miles, Merritt Lake at 12.5 miles, and Horseshoe Lake at 12.9 miles. Meet back up with the Six Lakes Trail after 15.0 miles; turn right and continue back to the trailhead at 20.1 miles.

OBSIDIAN FALLS (hike 90)

Trail length: About 5.5 miles one-way.
Description: A long day hike or a backpack trip in the Three Sisters Wilderness.
Difficulty: Moderate to strenuous.
Highlights: Wildflowers; waterfall.
Elevations: 4,800 to 6,400 feet.

Pages 78-79: View from the top of South Sister, Three Sisters Wilderness.
Below: Obsidian Falls, Three Sisters Wilderness.

Mink Lake, Three Sisters Wilderness.

Maps: Three Sisters Wilderness map.
Hiking season: July through October.
Permits: Wilderness Permit; Trail Park Permit.
Contact: McKenzie Ranger District, State Highway 126, McKenzie Bridge, OR 97413; (541) 822-3381.
Directions: From McKenzie Bridge, drive east on Oregon Highway 126; after 4.8 miles reach the junction of Oregon Highways. 126 and 242. Go right on Oregon 242, which is closed during the winter. (Check with the Forest Service for opening dates.) After 15.3 miles reach Forest Road 250; drive 0.3 mile to the trailhead.
Trail info: Hike Obsidian Trail 3528, reaching the junction of Spring Lake Trail 3528B at 0.8 mile. Keep straight to a lava flow at 2.9 miles. Enter the flow, noticing the nice views of Black Crater, Little Brother, North and Middle Sister, Belknap Crater, Little Belknap and Mt. Washington, along the way.

Cross White Branch Creek at 3.5 miles. The trail forks at the creek; keep to the right. Reach the Pacific Crest Trail (PCT) junction at 5.2 miles; go left to Obsidian Falls at 5.5 miles.

PROXY FALLS (hike 91)

Trail length: About 0.6 mile one-way.
Description: A day hike in the Three Sisters Wilderness.
Difficulty: Easy.
Highlights: Scenic waterfalls; wildflowers.
Elevations: 3,150 to 3,200 feet.
Maps: Three Sisters Wilderness map.
Hiking season: March through November.
Permits: Trail Park Permit.
Contact: McKenzie Ranger District, State Highway 126, McKenzie Bridge, OR 97413; (541) 822-3381.
Directions: Travel east on Oregon Highway 126 from McKenzie Bridge. After 4.8 miles reach the junction of Oregon Highways 126 and 242; turn right on Oregon 242, which is closed during the winter months. (The road is usually open sometime in June or July. Check with the Forest Service for opening dates.) Continue 8.8 miles to the trailhead.
Trail info: Hike Proxy Falls Trail 3532 through ancient lava flows where a vast array of wildflowers bloom in the spring. At 0.3 mile reach a junction; Upper Falls is located 0.1 mile to the left. Upper Proxy Falls tumbles down in two distinct cascades, spilling over mossy rocks into a deep pool.

From the junction, hike to Lower Falls, another 0.1 mile away.

There's a good view of Lower Proxy Falls from the railing. The 200 foot falls plunge down over mossy green stones, spraying mist outward and skyward, raining upon the surrounding plants 24 hours a day.

Viewing waterfalls such as these provide memories to last a life time. So others can experience the same beautiful memories, please remember to pack out all trash.

SOUTH SISTER (hike 92)

Trail length: About 6.7 miles one-way.
Description: A long day hike or a backpack trip in the Three Sisters Wilderness.
Difficulty: Strenuous.
Highlights: Scenic lake; spectacular views.
Elevations: 5,450 to 10,358 feet.
Maps: Three Sisters Wilderness map.
Hiking season: July through October.
Permits: Wilderness Permit; Trail Park Permit.
Contact: Bend Ranger District, 1230 NE 3rd, Bend, OR 97701; (541) 388-5664.
Directions: Reach the Green Lakes Trailhead by driving west from Bend via the Cascades Lakes Highway (Oregon Highway 46) for 27 miles. You'll see the large trailhead across the road from Sparks Lake.
Trail info: Moraine Lake is a popular base camp for those aiming for the top of South Sister, so I would recommend a long day hike. The lake is definitely overused.

Hike the Green Lakes Trail, paralleling Fall Creek until reaching a junction at 2.2 miles; make a left and continue until you reach Moraine Lake at 3.3 miles.

The route from Moraine Lake is not a technical climb, just a long, steep hike up the mountain. However, hikers should remember that this is a 10,000-foot mountain, subject to quick and sometimes violent weather changes, so pack accordingly. (Note: The climb is not technical in summer. If there is snow, bring ice axe and crampons and know how to use them.)

You'll see several unmaintained trails leading north from Moraine lake. Choose one and hike out of the flat basin. Although you will be traveling cross-country, it's quite easy to see where others have walked.

Reach the south end of Lewis Glacier at 5.3 miles. Head left and up the cinder-covered slopes, climbing the loose scree to the south end of the crater rim at 6.4 miles. Hike to the true summit at 6.7 miles.

INTRODUCTION TO
THE WALDO LAKE WILDERNESS

Numerous small lakes dot the land, sparkling like exquisite gems, shimmering in the sunlight. Pink rhododendrons bloom in early summer, brightening up many of the trails. Throughout the Waldo Lake Wilderness, old-growth pines and firs stand tall, reaching for the heavens.

Located about 20 miles east of Oakridge, the wilderness rests on the western slopes of the Oregon Cascades, in the Western Cascades and High Cascades province. Steep, dissected slopes are typical of the Western Cascades; moderate slopes and many lakes, meadows, and rock outcrops are symbolic of the High Cascades.

The preserve ranges in elevation from a low of 2,800 feet along the North Fork Willamette River to a high of 7,144 feet atop Fuji Mountain, a summit providing wonderful views into the entire area and points farther in the distance.

The concept for a wilderness began before 1970 with the North Waldo Study Plan. Years later, with the signing of the Oregon Wilderness Bill on June 26, 1984, the 39,200-acre preserve was established. The Willamette National Forest manages the area.

Named for Waldo Lake, one of the world's purest lakes and located just outside the eastern boundary, the area rests near the crest of the Cascade Mountains. Oregon's second largest lake spans more than 10 square miles, offers nearly 22 miles of shoreline, and rests at an elevation of 5,414 feet. The second deepest lake as well (at 1,932 feet, Crater Lake is the deepest), Waldo Lake reaches to a maximum depth of 420 feet.

Glacial activity has done much to shape the Waldo Lake Basin and surrounding areas. Researchers believe that about 12,000 years ago the area was the center of a large glacial cap, nearly 15,000 feet thick. Eventually the glacier melted, scraping and scooping out more than 800 lakes and potholes, including Waldo Lake which sits in a large glacial depression.

Red foxglove.

Old-growth forest, Waldo Lake Wilderness.

A trail leads 21.8 miles around lake itself, passing many beautiful sandy beaches along the way. The beaches are a result of the eruption of Mt. Mazama, a caldera which now holds Crater Lake. About 6,600 years ago the mountain erupted, depositing a two foot thick blanket of pumice over the area. According to researchers, "it was the silicates in this pumice that formed Waldo Lake's beautiful sandy beaches."

Wildlife is abundant in the area although most people do not see much of it. Roosevelt elk, black-tailed deer and black bear are common. Mule deer inhabit the east side of the Cascades, but intermingle with the black-tails near the crest of the Cascades. Cougar are rarely seen. Small mammals include squirrels, mink, marten, weasel, raccoon, bobcat, and coyote.

Bird life consists of bald eagles and osprey, seen near some of the lakes, as well as the usual jays, a variety of owls, and game birds such as blue and ruffed grouse.

An unwelcome form of insect life, the mosquito, is abundant from July through the first half of August. Hikers should use mosquito repellent. When the season is at its peak you may need a mosquito net.

While the Waldo Lake Wilderness is a popular place today, researchers believe the area has been "popular" for thousand of years. Stone tool artifacts found scattered throughout the area indicate "that Native Americans inhabited the area thousands of years before white settlers arrived."

White settlers of the late 1800's, early 1900's, found the Waldo area highly suitable for sheep grazing. During the same time, trappers also used the area to trap fur-bearing animals.

Long before the white man arrived, however, ancient western redcedars took hold, growing along the North Fork Willamette River. Today, some of the 800 year old giants stand alongside the Shale Ridge Trail. See WILLAMETTE RIVER for more information.

Hooded merganser (drake).

FUJI MOUNTAIN (hike 93)

Trail length: About 1.5 miles one-way.
Description: A day hike in the Waldo Lake Wilderness.
Difficulty: Moderate.
Highlights: Spectacular views; wildflowers.
Elevations: 6,200 to 7,144 feet.
Maps: Waldo Lake Wilderness map.
Hiking season: July through October.
Permits: Wilderness Permit; Trail Park Permit.
Contact: Oakridge Ranger District, 46375 Highway 58, Westfir, OR 97492; (541) 782-2291.
Directions: From Oakridge, drive 15.3 miles southeast via Oregon Highway 58 to Eagle Creek Road (Forest Road 5883). Head north on Road 5883, driving 10.7 miles to the trailhead.
Trail info: Hike Fuji Mountain Trail 3674 to a junction at 0.2 mile; the trail on the right leads to the South Waldo Shelter, and left to the top of Fuji Mountain. Stay left, reaching the top of the mountain at 1.5 miles.

LILLIAN FALLS (hike 94)

Trail length: About 1.2 miles one-way.
Description: A day hike in the Waldo Lake Wilderness.
Difficulty: Moderate.
Highlights: Waterfall; old-growth forest.
Elevations: 3,400 to 4,000 feet.
Maps: Waldo Lake Wilderness map.
Hiking season: May through November.
Permits: Wilderness Permit; Trail Park Permit.
Contact: Oakridge Ranger District, 46375 Highway 58, Westfir, OR 97492; (541) 782-2291.
Directions: From the only stop light in Oakridge, off Oregon Highway 58, go north then right, following the sign to Salmon Creek Road (which later becomes Forest Road 24). Travel 14.3 miles on Forest Road 24, then make a left on Forest Road 2421, going another 8.8 miles to the trailhead.
Trail info: Hike Black Creek Trail 3551, crossing several small streams before reaching Lillian Falls, a beautiful cascading waterfall located on Nettie Creek.

If you want to continue on to Waldo Lake you can continue on the trail to Klovdahl Bay, 2.6 miles away.

WALDO MOUNTAIN LOOP (hike 95)

Trail length: About 8.9 miles for the complete loop.
Description: A day hike in the Waldo Lake Wilderness.
Difficulty: Moderate to strenuous.
Highlights: Wonderful views; wildflowers.
Elevations: 4,400 to 6,357 feet.
Maps: Waldo Lake Wilderness map.
Hiking season: July through October.

Permits: Wilderness Permit; Trail Park Permit.
Contact: Oakridge Ranger District, 46375 Highway 58, Westfir, OR 97492; (541) 782-2291.
Directions: From the only stop light in Oakridge, off Oregon Highway 58, go north then right, following the sign to Salmon Creek Road (which later becomes Forest Road 24). Continue to Forest Road 2417 at 11.3 miles. Make a left, driving another 6.2 miles to Forest Road 2424. Go right, reaching the trailhead in 3.8 miles.
Trail info: Hike Salmon Lakes Trail 3585 to a fork in 300 feet or so; make a left, traveling Waldo Mountain Trail 3592. Reach another junction at 2.1 miles. Stay left on the Waldo Mountain Trail. You'll reach the summit and a lookout in another mile.

Head across the rocky ridge then descend to the junction of Winchester Ridge Trail 3596 at 4.0 miles. Stay straight, hiking to another junction at 4.5 miles; the loop continues to the right at this point, now traveling Wahanna Trail 3583. In 0.2 mile come to a junction; Waldo Lake is located down the trail to your left. Continue to Waldo Meadows via Salmon Lakes Trail 3585.

At 6.4 miles reach a junction to Cupit Mary Trail 3559. (The map may show this as Waldo Meadows Trail 3591.) Continue straight to the Waldo Mountain/Salmon Lakes junction at 8.9 miles; turn left and head back to the trailhead in 300 feet.

NORTH FORK WILLAMETTE RIVER (hike 96)

Trail length: About 2.5 miles one-way.
Description: A day hike in the Waldo Lake Wilderness.
Difficulty: Easy.
Highlights: Spectacular views; wildflowers.
Elevations: 3,000 to 3,100 feet.
Maps: Waldo Lake Wilderness map.
Hiking season: April through November.
Permits: Wilderness Permit; Trail Park Permit.
Contact: Oakridge Ranger District, 46375 Highway 58, Westfir, OR 97492; (541) 782-2291.
Directions: Reach the trailhead by driving from Westfir, a tiny town located just north of Oakridge off Oregon Highway 58. From there drive north on North Fork Road 19 for 30 miles to the marked trail head.
Trail info: Perfect for families, hike Shale Ridge Trail 3567, following an old road which now serves as a trail. In less than 2 miles you'll enter a grove of ancient western redcedars, some of which are more than 800 years old. Northwest Coast Indians used trees like these for totem poles, lodges, and canoes.

After about 2.5 miles you'll reach the North Fork Willamette River. Although the loveliest portion of the trail ends here, the trail does not; it merges with the Blair Lake Trail in another 3.8 miles. Continue the hike, if you so wish, by fording the river (crossing can be dangerous at times) and ascending the steep trail to Shale Ridge. The trail is a bit difficult to follow, but red ribbons mark the way.

Red-tailed hawk (adult).

INTRODUCTION TO THE WENAHA-TUCANNON WILDERNESS

Deep river canyons, broad tablelands, lava mesas and plateaus, and steep, sparsely vegetated valley walls, all combine to describe the rugged area known as the Wenaha-Tucannon Wilderness. If the area is visited sometime other than during the big game hunting season, solitude can also be found, as well as other sought-after wilderness values.

Located in northeast Oregon and southeast Washington, the wilderness consists of 177,412 acres, 66,417 acres of which lie in Oregon. Because this guidebook deals only with Oregon wilderness areas I've excluded any hikes found on the 110,995 acre Washington side.

The Umatilla National Forest manages the area, originally created by the Endangered American Wilderness Act of 1978. In 1957, the Regional Forester designated a portion of the wilderness—previously known as the Wenaha Back-Country and consisting of 99,000 acres—to provide an area in its undeveloped state for hunting, fishing, and camping. Later, in 1967, the Wenaha Back-Country area was enlarged to 111,244 acres and remained as such until inclusion in the Wenaha-Tucannon Wilderness.

Located in the Blue Mountains, the area ranges in elevation from a low of 2,000 feet along the Wenaha River to 6,401 feet atop Oregon Butte in Washington. Oregon's highest point appears to be an unnamed peak, rising 5,934 feet and located just south of the Oregon/Washington border on the west end of the wilderness.

American Indians first inhabited this area. In fact, many of the areas 203 miles of trail originated from paths chosen by the natives. Later, around the late 1800's, the trails were improved by cattlemen, sheepmen and trappers. Once the land was designated National Forest Land, trails were improved for fire control and grazing administration.

Today, elk hunters are the primary users of the trails. Those hunting or fishing in the wilderness should remember that the area is located in

Dragonfly.

two states. Hunting and fishing laws may vary according to the state.

A spring or summer visit is recommended. At this time of year, hikers and fishermen alike, are almost certainly guaranteed a true wilderness experience.

Summer temperatures (July through September) average about 80 degrees, but highs over 100 degrees are not uncommon. However, evenings are always cool, and pleasant for sleeping. Winter temperatures range from minus 20 degrees to 40 degrees above zero. Snowpack usually registers one to two feet along the Wenaha River, and eight to twelve feet at Oregon Butte.

A wide variety of trees dot the harsh terrain. Below 4,000 feet, hikers will mainly see a forest rich in Douglas-fir, western larch, grand fir, Engelmann spruce, and ponderosa pine. Above 4,000 feet, there exists primarily lodgepole pine and sub-alpine fir mixed with spruce, grand fir, and larch.

Canada geese (adult and goslings).

Wenaha River, Wenaha-Tucannon Wilderness.

Wildlife in the Wenaha-Tucannon abounds due to the variety of habitat. With patience and luck, one might see part of the concentration of Rocky Mountain Elk in the area. Also, there are mule deer. Along the Wenaha River and its principle tributaries is one of Oregon's and Washington's more successful populations of whitetail deer. Other year-round mammal inhabitants include the black bear, cougar, coyote, bobcat, marten, and numerous smaller species.

Birds abound, with regular sightings of both the bald and golden eagle. Also, there are goshawks, coopers and sharpshined hawks, great horned owls, barred owls, and an assortment of woodpeckers, song birds, and ruffed and blue grouse.

Rattlesnakes are common in the area, especially near the lower elevations along the river and when hiking off the trail. Hikers should use caution.

WENAHA RIVER (hike 97)

Trail length: About 4.5 miles one-way.
Description: A day hike or a backpack trip in the Wenaha-Tucannon Wilderness.
Difficulty: Moderate.
Highlights: Wildlife; solitude except during hunting season.
Elevations: 4,900 to 3,000 feet.
Maps: Wenaha-Tucannon Wilderness map.
Hiking season: June through November.
Permits: Trail Park Permit.
Contact: Umatilla National Forest, 2517 S.W. Hailey, Pendleton, OR 97801; (541) 276-3811.
Directions: Reach the Elk Flat Trailhead by driving from the small town of Troy toward Long Meadow. After 0.3 mile the road forks; turn right to Long Meadow on Forest Road 62 (Lookingglass-Troy Road). Travel 20.2 miles to a marked dirt road leading to Elk Flat; drive another 0.7 mile to the trailhead.
Trail info: Hiking trails typically ascend to the point of interest then descend back to the trailhead; this one descends to the river so you'll have to climb back to the trailhead. Several trails descend to the Wenaha River; this is probably one of the nicest.

Hike Elk Flat Trail 3241 to the confluence of the South Fork and North Fork Wenaha Rivers below. If you have energy to spare, you can hike Wenaha River Trail 6144, located on the opposite side of the river. Cross near the washed-out bridge and continue until you reach the well-maintained trail.

WENAHA RIVER/MILK CREEK (hike 98)

Trail length: About 4.1 miles one-way.
Description: A day hike or a backpack trip in the Wenaha-Tucannon Wilderness.
Difficulty: Moderate.
Highlights: Wildlife; solitude except during hunting season.
Elevations: 4,700 to 3,500 feet.
Maps: Wenaha-Tucannon Wilderness map.
Hiking season: June through November.
Permits: Trail Park Permit.
Contact: Umatilla National Forest, 2517 S.W. Hailey, Pendleton, OR 97801; (541) 276-3811.
Directions: There are two ways to reach the trailhead at Timothy Spring. From Troy, go south toward Long Meadow. The road forks at 0.3 mile; head to the right toward Long Meadow on Forest Road 62 (Lookingglass-Troy Road). Continue 25.1 miles to Forest Road 6413 and make a right; drive another 1.3 miles and turn right again, this time on Forest Road 6415. (This is a dirt road not recommended for two-wheel drive in wet weather.) Take this to Timothy Spring Campground, another 6.4 miles down the road. Turn right to enter the campground, driving to the trailhead and end of road in about 0.2 mile.

To reach the trailhead from the south, drive north from Elgin on Oregon Highway 204 for 20.1 miles; turn right on Forest Road 64. After 11.6 miles turn left on Forest Road 6411, driving to the junction of Forest Road 6403 at 1.7 miles. Turn right, driving 3.6 miles to Forest Road 6415; make a right and drive 4.4 miles to Timothy Spring Campground.
Trail info: Hike from the trailhead, crossing a stream and a creek before reaching a point near the South Fork Wenaha River at 2.0 miles. Ford the river another 100 yards down the trail and then cross several more creeks before reaching the South Fork Wenaha River/Milk Creek confluence at 4.1 miles.

Chukar.

INTRODUCTION TO
THE WILD ROGUE WILDERNESS

Cascading waterfalls, towering cliffs, rushing rapids, delicate wildflowers, abundant wildlife, and autumn colors all combine to make the Wild Rogue Wilderness a wonderful place to visit.

The Wild Rogue Wilderness is located in the southwest corner of Oregon with the southwest boundary near the small town of Agness.

The 36,000-acre wilderness was designated as such on February 24, 1978, when Congress passed the Endangered American Wilderness Act. Two government agencies manage the wilderness: the Siskiyou National Forest manages 26,500 acres, Bureau of Land Management 9,000 acres, and the remaining 500 acres are in private ownership.

There are two maintained trails found within the Wild Rogue Wilderness. The Panther Ridge trail follows pine and rhododendron-covered Panther Ridge, located in the northern section and leads to Hanging Rock, a rock that has been likened to Yosemite's Half Dome. It's an easy climb to the top of Hanging Rock (unlike Yosemite's Half Dome) where you'll see endless valleys and mountains and the Wild Rogue Wilderness beyond. See HANGING ROCK for details.

The Rogue River Trail parallels the famous Rogue River which flows through the heart of the wilderness. The 40-mile trail begins at Grave Creek and follows along the north bank of the river to Illahe. See ROGUE RIVER for directions on hiking the 15-mile section of trail located in the wilderness; this section stretches from Illahe to Marial.

Those visiting the Wild Rogue Wilderness should note that this wilderness is unlike others in that you'll find several lodges located along the river and motorboats are permitted on the Rogue River.

The Rogue River was designated a Wild and Scenic River in 1978. At that time, however, Congress demanded that the river continue to be managed under the Wild and Scenic River act of 1968. You will see and hear motorboats downstream from Blossom Bar, but a hike up the river is still worthwhile.

You'll find the best time to hike the trail is in the spring and fall thus avoiding the hot summer months, as well as the many rafting parties that camp along the river.

The Rogue River is nationally-known for it's tremendous fishing. It serves as a liquid highway to salmon and steelhead, anadromous fish which migrate up the river to gravel beds appropriate for spawning. Young fish then journey to the ocean to grow to maturity, returning to the Rogue River so the cycle may be repeated once again.

Wildlife lovers will enjoy the black-tailed deer which often walk right into camp. Black bear here and have been known to visit campsites. Incidents have occurred, so please use common sense and do not feed the wildlife. Other animals include otter, Roosevelt elk, raccoon, squirrels, and many more species.

Flora Dell Creek Waterfall Wild Rogue Wilderness.

An abundance of reptiles consist of lizards, skinks, newts, and salamanders, and on occasion you may see a ring-necked snake, king snake, rattlesnake, or Pacific pond turtle.

Birders might see great blue herons fishing along the river's edge and common mergansers zooming by. Water ouzels, also known as dippers, may be seen scurrying from rock to rock or plunging underwater in search of food. In addition, you may also see bald eagles, ospreys, blue grouse, hummingbirds, and many others.

Wildflowers do their part during the spring and early summer months by decorating the preserve with their bright colors and unique shapes. These flowers, along with the many plants and trees found in the area, will give any backpacker plenty to see, smell, and touch.

Don't touch the poison oak, though. Poison oak is common along portions of the Rogue River Trail, but can be avoided and shouldn't be a problem to those who can identify the plant. Another annoyance to be aware of are wood ticks and mosquitoes.

ROGUE RIVER (hike 99)

Trail length: About 15.0 miles one-way.
Description: A backpack trip in the Wild Rogue Wilderness.
Difficulty: Moderate.
Highlights: Exquisite streams; wildflowers; abundant wildlife; the wild Rogue River.
Elevations: 207 to 425 feet.
Maps: Wild Rogue Wilderness map.
Hiking season: Year-round, but spring and fall are best; it's hot in the summer, cold and rainy in winter.
Permits: Trail Park Permit.
Contact: Gold Beach Ranger District, 1225 S. Ellensburg, Gold Beach, OR 97444; (541) 247-6651.

Wood duck (drake).

Dew-covered spider web.

Directions: From Gold Beach, drive east on County Road 595 which later becomes Forest Road 33. The road follows the south bank of the famous Rogue River. Pass the small town of Agness 3 miles before crossing a bridge over the Rogue River, about 29 miles from Gold Beach. Follow the right fork (County Road 375) towards Illahe, reaching the Rogue River Trailhead sign 4 miles from the bridge.

Trail info: Hike Rogue River Trail 1160, a wonderful trail paralleling the mighty Rogue River for miles. (This guide includes the wilderness portion of the trail only.)

There are frequent views of the river as you hike to Solitude Bar at 7.7 miles. It's a good place from which to observe kayakers and rafters. The area, once an Indian village, was later famous for early-day gold mining.

Watch for poison oak and wood ticks as you hike. Reach Paradise Bar at 11.8 miles. It is a wild turkey management area, and dogs must remain leashed.

HANGING ROCK (hike 100)

Trail length: About 5.5 miles one-way.
Description: A long day hike in the Wild Rogue Wilderness.
Difficulty: Moderate, sometimes strenuous.
Highlights: Great views; wildflowers.
Elevations: 3,000 to 3,954 feet.
Maps: Wild Rogue Wilderness map.
Hiking season: Year-round, but can be closed by snow from time to time.
Permits: Trail Park Permit.
Contact: Gold Beach Ranger District, 1225 S. Ellensburg, Gold Beach, OR 97444; (541) 247-6651.
Directions: From Agness, go north on Forest Road 33 for 19 miles to the junction of Forest Road 3348. Turn right on Forest Road 3348 (towards Eden Valley) and continue two miles to Forest Road 5520; turn right again. After 2.6 miles turn right on Forest Road 050. (Some maps claim Road 054.) Stay on Road 050 to the "End of Road" sign. Turn right and park at the trailhead.
Trail info: Hike Panther Ridge Trail 1253 (actually an old jeep trail) a short ways to a junction; Bald Mountain Lookout is 3.8 miles to the west; turn left to reach Hanging Rock.

After 0.4 mile the road forks; take the right fork and at 3.7 miles you'll see Hanging Rock and the surrounding valley. Continue to 4.9 miles and the junction of Trail 1253A and Trail 1253. Trail 1253A leads to the Hanging Rock Trailhead, 0.3 mile away. Continue up Trail 1253 to Hanging Rock Trail at 5.3 miles. Follow the trail to Hanging Rock at 5.5 miles. Those who are not afraid of heights will find Hanging Rock a cinch to climb.
Special Note: Those who'd rather not hike the 5.5 mile trail recommended here, can reach the Hanging Rock Trailhead by driving on Road 5520 for another 4.3 miles. Turn right on Road No. 5520/140 and continue to the Hanging Rock Trailhead in 1.4 miles. Trail 1253A leads 0.3 mile to the junction of Trails 1253 and 1253A which are discussed in this text.

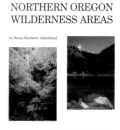

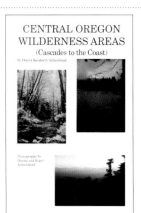

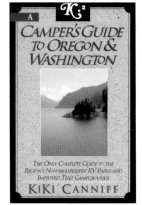